ABOUT THE AUTHOR

Praise for OVERCONNECTED

D1440569

1803484413

'*Overconnected* is a new, brilliant and provocative polemic on the miracle and curse of the Internet. And more. Chapter 5, "The Ghost in Our Midst", is on its own, invaluable. Read this if you're passionate about innovation, business, policy—or (just) the future.'

John Doerr, general partner, Kleiner Perkins
Caulfield & Byers, venture capital firm

'Bill, who oversaw the design of the original Intel microprocessor chip, has the courage to take a hard and honest look at the societal impact, both good and bad, of the technological revolution he himself helped start. Going further, Bill also offers sound solutions to some of the Internet's most dangerous excesses. This exciting new book is an essential read, making the strong case for ensuring ethical and pragmatic considerations always track technological innovation.'

Jean-Lou Chameau, President, California Institute of Technology

'As has been his wont in the past, Bill Davidow has once again put his finger squarely on the most salient risk in contemporary economic life. Earlier it was the rise of the virtual corporation (an idea Bill brought to the surface over *twenty years ago*). Now it is overconnectedness and all the issues of contagion it implies. Many big vision books are bunk. Bill's is the real deal. Let his thoughtfulness deepen your own.'

Geoffrey Moore, Author, *Crossing the Chasm*

'Bill Davidow has written a barn-burner of a thoroughly researched book loaded with interesting facts that reads like a novel describing how overconnectivity caused such catastrophes as the flash crash, day trading, cyber thieves, collateralized debt, mortgage meltdowns, credit defaults and the Icelandic catastrophe. He points out the need to adapt to the unintended consequences of the Internet and offers reasonable and thoughtful solutions.'

Arthur Rock, Venture Capitalist

OVERCONNECTED

What the Digital Economy
Says About Us

WILLIAM H. DAVIDOW

headline
business plus

First published in trade paperback in 2011
by HEADLINE PUBLISHING GROUP

First published in paperback in 2011
by HEADLINE PUBLISHING GROUP

1

Cataloguing in Publication Data is available from the British Library

ISBN 978 0 7553 6237 0

Offset in Fairfield by Avon DataSet Ltd,
Bidford-on-Avon, Warwickshire

Printed and bound by CPI Group (UK) Ltd, Croydon, CR0 4YY

Headline's policy is to use papers that are natural, renewable and
recyclable products and made from wood grown in sustainable forests.
The logging and manufacturing processes are expected to conform
to the environmental regulations of the country of origin.

HEADLINE PUBLISHING GROUP
An Hachette UK Company
338 Euston Road
London NW1 3BH

www.headline.co.uk
www.hachette.co.uk

To Sonja, the creator of my wonderful life and family

Contents

Acknowledgments

Over the years, many people have challenged, supported, and encouraged me. It would not have been possible to write this book without them.

Katie Hafner made this book possible. She contributed ideas, and researched and wrote much of the book. In many ways it is as much hers as mine.

None of this would have happened without the support of Cecile Engel, my publisher, who encouraged me to rewrite the manuscript one more time after I had put prior drafts in a drawer. My editor, Christopher Lehmann-Haupt, devoted endless hours to the project and greatly improved the book's readability. Tom Parker also supported me through the writing process. Over the past several years, James Levine, my agent, read the manuscript in its many iterations. Kimberly Summe generously read the book in various stages of completion. Alda Sigmundsdóttir was invaluable to the book, conducting research from Iceland. Two of my closest friends and most enthusiastic supporters are no longer with us. Russ Berg read almost every word I wrote and continually provided me with new perspectives. My remarkable friend Tory Atkins learned about the book late in his life, took a deep interest in the project, and introduced me to my publisher. Without their encouragement and interest, this project would have never been completed.

Faculty members at the Berkeley Round Table on International Economics (BRIE), located at the University of California, Berkeley, spent a great deal of time critiquing and reviewing my ideas. I am deeply indebted to Stephen Cohen and Brad DeLong for the effort they expended on my behalf. John Zysman, Constantine Magin, and Alberto Di Minin all contributed as well.

A number of friends at the Santa Fe Institute helped point me in the right direction. W. Brian Arthur spent hours discussing the topic with me, and his writings provided many of the early clues. John Padgett suggested that many of the answers I was looking for would come from the study of cities. He was right. Walter Fontana helped me sort out several issues. When you visit the Santa Fe Institute you meet many interesting people. I greatly benefited from discussions with Marcus Feldman, Harold Morowitz, Sam Bowles, Cormac McCarthy, Doyne Farmer, Juris Hartmanis, and many others.

Members of the faculty at the Stanford Institute for Economic Policy Research (SIEPR) provided many useful insights. I am especially indebted to two wonderful economic historians—Paul David and Nathan Rosenberg, whose work influenced me greatly. John Shoven, the director of SIEPR, took a continuing interest in the project. Bruce Owen spent considerable time helping me with publishers. I benefited from discussions with a number of others who are members of the SIEPR group—Kenneth Arrow, Michael Boskin, Timothy Bresnahan, Edward Lazear, Roger Noll, Paul Romer, James Sweeney, John Taylor, and Gregory Rosston.

I am especially grateful to Cullen Murphy, former editor of *The Atlantic*, who took an interest in this project and pointed me to normal accidents. Charles Perrow wrote the seminal work in that field. Both his writing and critiques have shaped many of the ideas in the book.

A number of members of the Caltech faculty provided me with ideas and a better understanding of the key issues I faced. I am especially indebted to Joel Franklin, who caught a critical error in my thinking. John Doyle educated me about the dangers of interconnections introducing undesirable influences into control structures, and numerous discussions with John Ledyard focused my thoughts. And my good friend Tom Tombrello challenged me at every turn and forced me to dig deeper to answer his criticisms.

In the process of working on this project, I met some wonderful people who were kind enough to spend time with me and provide advice. John Staudenmaier, an expert on the history of technology, pointed me to some great historical texts, which convinced me that much of what I was writing about had happened before in a slightly different form. Discussions with Joel Mokyr, and reading his work, opened my eyes to the parallels between the Industrial Revolution and the advent of the Internet. John Seeley Brown and Paul Saffo were great sounding boards. My good friends Igor Khandros, Buno Pati, Vaughn Walker, and Geoffrey Moore provided many useful insights.

This book became a Sisyphean task. Just when I thought I had completed it, a new idea materialized and the manuscript rolled back down the hill for another rewrite. Over the years that have gone into writing this book, I have lost track of some of those who helped. I apologize to those I've overlooked as a result of my failure to keep good records.

OVERCONNECTED

Introduction: New Lessons
from the Internet

In 2007 I attended a lecture by Buzz McCoy, a financier who had directed Morgan Stanley's real estate finance activities for more than a dozen years. Feeling mischievous in a room filled with economists, investors, and others who knew their stuff, I stood up and spoke out, blaming—of all things!—the Internet for the emerging real estate crisis. Laughter rippled through the room as I made the case that the Internet had created a world where speed erases the ability to reflect, where investors act in haste, driven by fear that others will snap up the best deals, where ill-considered investments are fueled by easy money. However, as I spoke, the laughter died down and heads began nodding. One person came up to me afterward to tell me about a $75 million deal he was involved with that closed in the passion of the moment.

By 2007, the Internet had become so much a part of our way of life that we were no longer conscious of the ways it was affecting us. We all knew we were getting information instantly, passing documents around through the ether, getting our news almost simultaneously as events occurred, sending documents as e-mail attachments that we could attach an electronic signature to, closing deals and conducting business with individuals and institutions that we had met only in virtual space. But we were not conscious of how all this was affecting our institutions, our emotions, our judgment, and our levels of trust.

•

A seismic illustration of the Internet's influence occurred in February 2006, when freedom of expression collided head-on with radical Islam. Several months earlier, a Danish newspaper printed 12 caricatures of the prophet Muhammad. Many of the cartoons were unambiguously provocative. One depicted Muhammad as a terrorist with a stick of dynamite in his turban; in another, instead of dynamite in the turban it was a pair of horns; still another showed him astride a cloud, greeting suicide bombers as they arrived in the hereafter.

Although many newspapers refused to reprint the cartoons, the drawings quickly landed on the Internet and circled the globe in seconds. Chaos erupted. Peaceful protests exploded into riots. Danish embassies in Syria, Lebanon, and Iran were set on fire. Forty thousand angry Pakistanis demonstrated in Karachi and burned the Danish prime minister in effigy. At least 139 people died. Pakistani cleric Maulana Yousaf Qureshi put a $1 million bounty on the head of Kurt Westergaard, one of the illustrators.

The violence that resulted from the online, flulike spread of a controversial set of cartoons is an extreme example of what I call overconnectivity, a concept that serves as both the leitmotif and the lesson of this book. By "overconnected" I mean what happens to a system when connectivity increases dramatically both inside and outside of it, and parts, if not the whole system, are unable to adjust. When that happens, a situation can easily spin out of control. In the case of the Muhammad cartoons, the Internet played an important role in stirring anger and violence, not only in its role as conduit for the drawings themselves but also by helping to spread the angry commentary that followed in their wake. Sometimes overconnectivity leads to violence. Sometimes it triggers serious accidents. Sometimes it takes a company—or country—to the brink of bankruptcy.

When I talk with people about overconnectivity, most wrongly assume I am referring to the overabundance of technology in our lives. Indeed, we are all too aware of the nagging buzz of iPhones and BlackBerries as they disrupt meetings, meals, and movies with their never-ending stream of e-mails, instant messages, and tweets. This book, by contrast, is about human behavior—how the actions society takes have become so complex and interwoven that the simplest ones have effects far beyond what we imagine.

When the seventeenth-century poet and clergyman John Donne wrote his famous line "No man is an island," he continued, "Every man is a piece of the continent, a part of the main." He was writing at a time when the most important interconnections were still local. If Donne were to write those words today, he might say, "Every man is a piece of the world." What happened on a local or regional basis in the past is now occurring globally. We no longer coevolve with just our neighbors; we coevolve with the world.

Connections can be loose and weak or tight and powerful. Some connections are so weak they don't matter. If two people live in neighboring houses but never talk, they are very weakly connected. If two Americans live a thousand miles apart, they are connected because they are both U.S. citizens, but the connection is still very weak. If they both join a white supremacist group, they become more tightly connected. If they start interacting over a Web site for white supremacists, the connection becomes stronger still.

Three hundred million people live in the United States, and we are all connected to one another in some way. In the 2008 presidential election, more than sixty-seven million people voted for Barack Obama. All of them believed he was the best candidate, and all were connected by that common cause. For many, that single vote marked the beginning and end of their bond. Others became strongly connected to one another by working together on the campaign. It was those strong connections, in the end, that created the momentum that got Obama elected.

One person who could not have foreseen the unprecedented level of interconnectivity that permeates society today is William Ogburn, the early-twentieth-century sociologist who coined the term "cultural lag" to describe the social misalignment that occurs when one element of a culture changes and other elements don't. Although Ogburn was no Luddite, he pointed out how painful the adjustment process to technological advance could be, and he concluded that to slow down such advance might be beneficial, if only to forestall the revolution-ary upheaval that too rapid progress has the potential to inflict on society.

When I first read Ogburn's work, his ideas struck me as alarm-ist. To a technologist like myself, the very notion of slowing the pace of technological progress was heresy. And the idea of technology triggering revolution seemed fanciful at best. But then, in late 2005, when the Internet brought the Muslim world into direct con-tact with Danish political satire and deadly riots broke out around the world the next year, Ogburn's ideas did not sound so far-fetched after all.

If the interaction of technology and social upheaval was William Ogburn's concern in the 1920s, one can only imagine, especially in light of the sheer ubiquitousness of the Internet, what he would think of the cultural lag in today's society. In fact, we are no longer facing a mere lag, a term too benign for our situation. In Ogburn's day, change was slow compared with today's change, when, driven by the Internet, it is instantaneous.

As I reflected on the impact of the Internet, I came to realize that our economic and social institutions reflect the environment to which they are connected. As connectivity changes, institutions transform themselves to take advantage of those changes. In the nineteenth century, factories grew bigger because the railroad enabled them to serve larger markets. Today, equally dramatic changes are occurring because of the Internet.

One goal for this book is to explain how overconnected environ-ments perform, how they feed upon themselves and become unpre-dictable, accident-prone, and subject to contagions. As you will see, overconnectivity has placed many parts of our lives—and the planet—precariously balanced on a knife's edge.

The potential for unexpected catastrophe is nothing new; the tulip mania that gripped Holland in the early seventeenth century, running up the prices of tulip bulbs to insane heights only to have them crash back down, is certainly one instance of that. But what is different now is the heightened interconnectivity caused by the Internet—the most effective connection machine in the history of humankind—and the bête noire in this book.

Since its unprepossessing origins nearly four decades ago as an academic experiment, the Internet has become the medium in which much of advanced global society now functions. And it caught on quickly—from 10 million users in 1995 to an estimated 1.9 billion in 2010. Its reach was broad: it spanned the world and affected people in the most developed and the least developed countries. It revolutionized communication. It was fast, cheap, reliable, and easy to use.

But in an overconnected world, the interdependencies spawned by the Internet let problems grow and spread so that the span of government controls, of checks and balances normally built into a system, no longer matches the domain of the problem. Identity thieves operating in less developed countries and beyond the reach of law enforcement agencies steal money from citizens in developed ones. Pornographic material that is legal in California circulates in Tennessee, where it is against the law. Internet gambling casinos, legal in Great Britain, collect wagers from Texas, where the practice is illegal.

Stronger connections, it turns out, have only magnified the problems, turning local problems into national ones and national crises into international ones Now, as all other forms of interconnections have improved, and as those interconnections have grown more robust thanks to the Internet, society is increasingly subject to interdependencies—not always for the better.

At no time was this interdependency made clearer than during the economic crisis of 2008. Forget the "collateralized debt obligations," "credit default swaps," and other financial terms of baffling intricacy you've heard associated with the crash. All of them played a role, for sure. But none of them, alone, was responsible for the enormity of the financial disaster. I can tell you without a shred of doubt that this mother of all financial crises was largely a result of overconnectivity.

U.S. treasury secretary Timothy Geithner summed up the problem when he appeared before Congress on June 19, 2009. Geithner noted that the overconnected banking system "magnified risk." When things went sour, the impact was enormous: "The resulting damage on Wall Street hit Main Streets across the country, affecting virtually every American."

Of course, the Internet did not cause the global economic crisis; cheap money, lax regulation, and unchecked avarice did. What the Internet did was act as an accelerant, spreading information very quickly. It was gasoline on the flames. A crisis of this dimension would not have been possible without a very efficient, fast, cheap, and reliable information transportation system. Across the worldwide digital sprawl, things go viral at lightning speed. And people were carried away in a competitive, greedy fervor of their own creation.

I wasn't always such an alarmist. For many years I believed that heightened interaction and enhanced access to information were good. As a venture capitalist for more than two decades, and a technology executive for even longer, I witnessed firsthand the ushering in of the Internet era. And like so many other optimists in Silicon Valley, I assumed we were headed in an increasingly positive direction—that the more information we had, and the more people could interact with one another, the better. After all, wasn't all this bringing new efficiencies to business and greater transparency to government? Wasn't it delivering vital information to remote villages in developing countries and providing new levels of freedom to people everywhere? Wasn't it creating economic prosperity and jobs?

Then, in 2000, when the market for tech stocks imploded, I began to wonder about the speed with which the irrational exuberance had driven up the price of technology stocks. Much of that exuberance had been driven by hype in online discussion forums and by day traders who used the Internet to gather information, spread rumors, and do their trading. What, I asked myself, is going on here?

I became, if not exactly skeptical, then definitely more curious about the potentially disruptive impact of a networked world. What I soon discovered was that the unintended consequences of this onrush of interconnectivity were by no means all positive. I began to wonder how our tightly interconnected environment was affecting the institutions we have long relied on to run our governments, our economy, and our society. I realized that much of our society is overconnected. The result has been a high degree of disruption in the established way of the world. Many businesses that looked as if they would live forever were being transformed or driven into bankruptcy. Rock-solid financial institutions were turning to the government to bail them out. Governments were struggling with tax systems, copyright laws, Internet gambling, and legal jurisdiction. What was not legal in one country was fine in another. When things moved to cyberspace, who governed?

Paradoxically enough, when the mortgage crisis seemed at its worst, I started to become an optimist again. I noticed that people were tearing up the old book of rules and starting to play by new ones as they grew increasingly sensitive to the new environment. People started acting to close the cultural gap Ogburn had written about. They began to respond to the effects of overconnectivity even though they did not fully comprehend what was driving the situation. Even if they didn't understand that the Internet was part of the problem, they knew the world was becoming more volatile, changing at an accelerated pace, and being driven to extremes.

People were beginning to question Alan Greenspan's long-standing disdain for regulation and the lack of federal constraints on financial firms. In 2008, after being devastated by the crisis, people began to express growing concern over this absence of regulation. Suddenly they began to understand the dangers posed by institutions such as AIG and Citigroup, institutions that were too big to fail. They might not have understood the role that overconnectivity and the Internet played in creating them, but they were coming to grips with the problems such institutions created. And in my own circles I began to detect more willingness to consider changing the system in ways that would better align it with the rapid rate of technological change. Maybe cultural lag was something we were learning to compress and in some instances even eliminate.

Which brings me to the final goal of this book, after persuading you that we're overconnected and explaining what happens when we are—to suggest ways to avoid the effects of overconnectivity, by reducing the number of extreme events and lessening their impact. I'll look at potential changes in our approach to policy making, with an eye toward reengineering aspects of government, the economy, and our social institutions.

I now firmly believe that if we play by new rules we can greatly benefit from the dramatic increase in interconnectivity we now live with. But if we ignore the potential for new rules we will experience more meltdowns, at an accelerated pace.

It is impossible to really understand what went on in the worldwide economic crisis of 2008 without examining the role that the Internet played in supercharging it. Without the Internet, the credit mess would have undoubtedly caused a recession of some magnitude. While we can never measure the Internet's full effects, we know that it made the current crisis larger, more widespread, and more virulent. It not only carried the information, it also helped spread what is known as a "thought contagion." That is, the rate at which greed and fearmongering took place—via instant access to news and online rumors—was accelerated to unprecedented levels.

The ideas that propel this book will reveal themselves through stories about great industrial cities, such as Chicago and Pittsburgh.

I will discuss how interconnections have caused crop failure in Bali and the loss of our privacy. I will tell you about financial accidents and contagions—about the 1987 stock market crash, about the recent severe recession, and about John Law's creative swindle that devastated the wealth of French royalty while at the same time creating an inflationary spiral that led to a popular distrust of paper money and kept France financially backward for generations. And I will be taking readers across some unlikely terrain. Some of it may seem utterly obvious, while some will seem counterintuitive, if not entirely far-fetched. You will hear of the growth of monopolies and of online bankers in Reykjavík, Iceland.

In the end, this book maps a journey reflecting my own path from buoyant optimist to studied skeptic and back full circle to optimist. Some readers will think I have placed too much of the blame for our current woes on an intrinsically benign collection of communications protocols and data switches: "Gee, Officer, the Internet made me do it." But even conceding the impossibility of measuring the Internet's contribution, I insist that the Internet accelerated and amplified whatever fundamental factors were already in place. In a very real sense, the Internet did indeed make us do it.

ONE

What the Steam Engine Can Teach Us about the Internet

I grew up in a small Chicago suburb in the 1940s. On cold winter evenings, my mother would drive us to meet my father's train from the city. At the station, she would sit in the warm car with the engine running while I jumped out into the freezing cold and ran along the platform, hoping to spot the headlight of the approaching locomotive. Eventually, it would appear in the distance, growing brighter, the roar of the engine getting louder. Smoke streamed from the train's stack, quickly lost to the darkness. Finally, the massive black locomotive, its iron brakes pressing against giant drive wheels, would screech, then wheeze to a halt a few feet from where I stood. The smell of steam escaping from the locomotive's pistons filled the night air as my father stepped from the passenger coach, his arms open in greeting. Holding his hand as we walked along the platform, I'd hear first one chug and then the next as the train pulled out of the station. Watching the red taillight recede, I'd often wonder, safe in my father's grip, where that red light would stop next.

My father appreciated my infatuation with the railroad, and he used it as an opportunity to teach me a few things. He once pointed out that no rail line actually ran continuously through Chicago itself. Despite the fact that hundreds of trains ran into and out of the city every day, all freight—and passengers—passing through the city from any direction had to stop in Chicago and be transferred from one line to another. Chicago was a choke point. That, my father insisted, was why Chicago was so important.

By the early nineteenth century, Chicago was already rich with interconnections. Even before the railroad, canals, rivers, lakes, and dirt roads linked the city to its local environs and ultimately to distant cities in the United States and around the world, prompting the city's boosters in the 1840s to proclaim Chicago "the most important point in the Great West." All roads west seemed to converge on the city. Over the next fifty years many of these inefficient methods of interconnecting were replaced by the railroad, whose arrival drove the transformation of business and the natural environment of the entire Midwest.

One of my favorite stories about enterprise involves Gustavus Swift, the nineteenth-century Chicago meatpacker who invented the refrigerated railcar. He did so out of sheer necessity. Back then, meat processing was a breathtakingly inefficient business. Cattle were raised on the prairies and driven by cowboys to railheads in places such as Dodge City, Kansas, then shipped to the markets in the Midwest and on the East Coast. The system provided an object lesson in inefficiency. Cattle lost weight during the shipping process, many were injured and died, and much of the animal, the innards, for example, had little or no market value.

Swift decided to try something both radical and risky. He reversed the order of things by first slaughtering and dressing the beef in his slaughterhouses. He put refrigeration in his railcars, then hung the carcasses vertically. The new approach solved a host of problems. Swift reduced his shipping costs because he could fit many more vertical carcasses in a car than he could live head of cattle. What's more, he was shipping only those products that had value on the market.

Swift's strategy transformed the butchering business on the East Coast. The butchers could not compete with Swift's efficient slaughterhouses. Swift's innovative means of shipping, enabled by the rail network, had put the eastern businesses in direct competition with a more efficient competitor a thousand miles away. The local butchers had higher slaughtering costs than Swift. If they shipped live cattle to the East Coast from Chicago, they incurred higher shipping costs as well. The butchers were forced to restructure their business. Many stopped slaughtering their own cattle and cut up Swift's carcasses into steaks and roasts for customers.

Before long, Swift had become the largest meatpacker in the country. Through the use of a new form of connectivity he had restructured the meat-processing industry. So the refrigerated railcar had some effects very similar to those the Internet has had on businesses today. In short, physical connectivity was restructuring business long before the Internet existed. It was changing the role of local butcher shops just as the Internet has reduced the importance of travel agents.

My father died in 1989, long before the Internet exploded into society's collective consciousness. But he definitely knew how to impart lessons that would stick, because it wasn't until I studied the evolution of the railroad that I began to comprehend the speed with which the Internet affected life in the late twentieth century.

By the early 1900s, railroad lines radiated out from Chicago like the spokes of a great wheel. Travel time between New York and Chicago shrank from almost three weeks by stagecoach to two days. Within a few decades, Chicago's reach had widened to encircle the prairies, the northern woods, and the markets on the East Coast, creating an ecosystem that was both driven and supported by the railroad, with Chicago at its center.

Meatpacking was only one industry affected by the railroad. Agriculture was another. Before the arrival of the railroad, farmers sent burlap bags of grain to Chicago warehouses in wagons that traveled on dirt roads. The farmers retained ownership of individual bags full of grain that were stored in the warehouses, which created a logistical and accounting nightmare as the volume of transactions grew.

In response, the city built grain elevators in which to store grain in bulk. As the grain trade expanded, the Chicago Board of Trade established uniform quality standards that made it possible to safely mix the grain from a variety of farms in the storage buildings and offer it for sale. Thus did a railroad become associated with the creation of one of the most important financial derivatives* of the twentieth century—commodity futures. Farmers were given receipts for their output, which they could then sell, often to speculators, who would try to turn an additional profit. This speculative buying and selling, streamlined by powerful new ways to interconnect—the railroads and the telegraph—ultimately led to the emergence of a thriving Chicago-based futures market.

In the process, the old ways of doing business vanished, and new, efficient business models better suited to the more connected environment emerged. More effective rail connections made it easier to get grain to the market and cattle to the stockyards. This rail network led to explosive growth in the prairie states and a growing demand for lumber to build homes, barns, and fences. Without forests to meet that demand, prairie farmers turned to their neighbors in the north; indeed, the future of the prairie farmer soon came to depend on the cutting of the northern forests. In short order, Chicago became the hub of a thriving lumber market. Pine from the northern forests was arriving from the north by ship and train, and the railroads carried it to the prairies, filling railcars that once had been empty on their trips west.

The general stores that had served the needs of the prairie farmers and ranchers were now being bypassed and became vulnerable to competition from catalog retailers, whose products could be shipped by rail. Geographically dispersed customers could order a wide variety of low-priced goods from thick catalogs, giving rise to Chicago's

---

*A derivative is a financial contract between two or more parties, the value of which is determined by the fluctuations of an underlying asset. Common underlying assets include stocks, bonds, commodities, currencies, interest rates, and market indexes.

great catalog merchandisers, the world's first major "virtual" retailers. The catalogs arrived in prairie towns by train, which served as a nineteenth-century version of high-bandwidth connection. Sears, Roebuck and Montgomery Ward, the Amazon.coms of their day, supplied tools, furniture, and other merchandise, first to farmers and woodsmen and, ultimately, to an entire nation.

As the farmers and those who served and supplied them prospered, so did Chicago as a whole. The city's population mushroomed from fewer than 30,000 in 1850 to more than 1.5 million by the turn of the century. Chicago became a crucible for entrepreneurs and innovators, a major center of manufacturing and commerce. Cyrus McCormick grew wealthy from his mechanical reapers, George Pullman from his sleeping cars.

Also in the nineteenth century, not only did the cost of physical connections fall rapidly, but also the cost of moving information: the expense of printing and shipping catalogs and books decreased and, more crucially, the telegraph system began carrying a greater load of vital information.

Then came some simple synergy. It turned out that when you combined an information link (the telegraph) with a physical link (the railroad), the combination made the physical connection much more powerful. For one thing, the information made the railroads both safer and more efficient. Since many of the rail lines were single tracked, knowing what was coming the other way was of vital importance in avoiding crashes. Also, the telegraph allowed farmers to figure out where the price for certain crops was the highest. Using this information, farmers could ship their products to markets where the demand was greatest. And the rapid transfer of information was critical to managing the railroads efficiently—the telegraph enabled managers to know where the railcars themselves were at any given time, so they could be kept loaded with freight.

At first glance, a massive black steam engine pulling a long chain of railcars on iron tracks does not appear to have much in common with bits chasing one another at the speed of light through fiber-optic cables. But I can assure you it does. The railroad was, in its time, a powerful new form of connectivity. It enabled the creation of new financial products and allowed data-rich catalogs to be shipped to customers. In conjunction with the telegraph, the railroad improved farmers' access to markets and made those markets more efficient— transforming cities and prairies alike.

TWO

Overconnectivity and Surprises

The changes brought by the railroad happened over several decades. It took a long time to build bridges and lay tracks. It took years to improve the efficiency of steam engines. New materials had to be developed to enable boilers to handle high pressure. New tools were needed to fabricate the boilers from those new materials. Low-cost steel was required to make rails durable enough to bear heavy loads. In the end, rail systems created faster, cheaper connections between distant locations, and transformation followed.

By contrast, the Internet's dramatic effect on interconnectivity seemed to happen in a flash—so fast indeed that we have lost control of it. How did this happen? How did this particular skein of interconnections we are living with now grow so tangled? How is it that the same technology allowing us to pay our bills online makes us fear that our identity will be stolen out from under us? How did the very network that allows families to go online to shop for both a house and a mortgage also become the conduit for a series of transactions that would eventually cause them to lose that house and default on the mortgage? And what are we to do?

To answer such questions, one has to understand the dynamics of networks and connectivity in the postindustrial age, particularly instances of systems that cannot adjust when their level of connectivity reaches a certain threshold—or what might be referred to simply as overconnectivity. Overconnected environments tend to be very unstable and are subject not just to very rapid change but also to accidents, as a paper written in 1958 by Eugene Wigner, the Princeton mathematician, demonstrates. Wigner shows that under certain conditions particular types of large, interconnected physical systems will always be unstable. As a system increases in size and the interconnections strengthen, the probability that instabilities will occur increases. The equations Wigner analyzes are very similar to the ones economists use to analyze economic systems. Wigner's paper is complemented by one written in 1970 by the British cyberneticist W. Ross Ashby, which concludes that "all large complex dynamic systems may be expected to show the property of being stable up to a critical level of connectance, and then, as connectance increases, to go suddenly unstable." Of course, this is precisely what happens if you pull the control rods out too far on a nuclear reactor or bring together a critical mass of uranium in an atom bomb. The reactor melts down, and the bomb explodes.

A rapid increase in interconnectivity has the potential to do two things. First, it can drive change at very rapid rates, so rapid that, as William Ogburn, in defining the term "cultural lag" wrote, "an element of a culture that was in step with its environs changes and the environs are unable to keep up." Technological change, driven in part by the increases in interconnections, has the ability to create new institutions, and the environment frequently lacks the ability to accommodate them. This inability of the environment to keep up with technological change means that overconnectivity has the ability to create a great deal of cultural lag. Second, our environment is composed of the things we are connected to, so if dramatic increases in the levels of connectivity abruptly change the things we are connected to, then our institutions undergo rapid environmental change. Unless the institution is exceedingly nimble, it cannot keep up with changes in its environs. Once again, the result is a great deal of cultural lag.

•

When it comes to degrees of connectivity, there are four general classifications that can be applied to nations, economic regions, and societies:

1. Underconnected state. Isolated ancient civilizations, primitive cultures, and undeveloped countries are examples of underconnected states. The environment around them might be changing and they wouldn't know it, while endogenous change is extremely slow or nonexistent. When and if these cultures become connected to new environments, they experience a large shock; the resulting cultural lag can be devastating. Primitive aboriginal cultures are destroyed when they come in contact with the modern world. Of course, there are modern societies that are underconnected as well. Iceland, a country I was to become fascinated by, existed in a state of underconnection until well into the twentieth century.

2. Interconnected state. In this state, when the environment changes gradually, businesses, economic systems, and govern-ments are capable of keeping pace. As long as the environment doesn't change too abruptly, these institutions are comfortable and can keep up. On the other hand, if the institutions change first and do so gradually, they will drive changes in the environment. When this happens, the environment has time to change and can accommodate the institutions. There is little or no cultural lag. Chicago before the railroad, for instance, existed in an interconnected state.

3. Highly connected state. This is a critical level of connectivity that appears to make everything go right. In many cases, a high level of connectivity is intimately related to success. In this state, businesses, economic systems, and

government institutions are driving change. The environment in which they are embedded might struggle to keep up, but it is able to do so with a minimal level of disruption. The flip side of this state is that the increase in interconnections can cause rapid change in the environment, but if the institutions are flexible they can stay in step. There is a challenging level of cultural lag, but society can still cope and prosper. Silicon Valley in the late twentieth century and Chicago in the early twentieth century are examples of economic areas that prospered in a highly connected state.

4. Overconnected state. In this state, institutions change so quickly that the environment in which they are embedded is unable to cope. Or the reverse happens: with the increase in interconnections, the environment changes so dramatically that the institutions become overwhelmed by cultural lag and are unable to cope. In this book, Iceland is the case I examine most closely apropos of this state.

Of course, there are no clear lines separating these categories. In a highly connected environment, an investment bank can start conducting business differently and prosper as a result, then outrun the regulatory environment and spin out of control. If enough financial institutions do the same thing, the economy finds itself in an overconnected state, and chaos follows. Sometimes overconnectivity is a result of both rapid endogenous change and a simultaneous change in the external environment. Iceland underwent a large increase in interconnections that not only drove rapid change within it but also connected it to a new environment—the world of international finance—to which the country found itself ill equipped to adapt.

Before the railroad, Chicago was connected to its environs by canals, dirt roads, and shipping on Lake Michigan. The interconnections were weak. With the introduction of the railroad, Chicago became deeply embedded in a new environment, which consisted of the north woods, the farms out on the prairies, and the markets on the East Coast. There was rapid environmental change. The institutions in Chicago leveraged the interconnections and changed rapidly as well. The commodities market emerged to handle the large growth in the volume of grain shipments. Retailers became catalog merchandisers to supply products to the prairies. Gustavus Swift invented his new method of processing beef, which took advantage of refrigerated railcars that he developed to service eastern markets. McCormick built his reapers to supply the farms, and Pullman provided his railcars. Chicago entered a new state: it became highly connected, and beneficially so.

The newspaper industry, on the other hand, has recently had the misfortune of departing from a connected state, bypassing a highly connected state altogether, and landing directly in an overconnected one. For years, newspapers prospered in a stable, connected state. The amount of advertising determined the size of the "news hole," which in turn got filled by a staff of reporters and photographers and wire services such as the Associated Press and United Press International. Every night, like clockwork, the newspapers were printed on large printing presses, and at dawn paperboys tossed them onto lawns.

The Internet changed both the newspapers and the means of delivery. News that once appeared on paper was now delivered over the Internet. Almost overnight, newspapers went from thriving in an interconnected environment to suffering in an overconnected one. People stopped reading print newspapers, advertisers disappeared, and circulation plummeted. Unable to cope, some newspapers began abandoning their print product and switched to Web-only news. Others struggled to adopt new business models. The current chaos in the industry is a sign of overconnection.

What does it take for an institution that seemed rock solid to dissolve into some new, unanticipated state? Often the cause is positive feedback.

When most people hear the term "positive feedback," they tend to think that positive feedback brings exclusively happy results (dog rolls over on command, receives praise and a treat) and that negative feedback means just the opposite—unhappy results (kid gets scolded for a bad grade, kicks the innocent dog, goes to his room, and slams the door). But those are actually examples of positive and negative *reinforcement*. I am using feedback in the sense that engineers—and I confess to being one—use it, the term "positive" referring to the fact that change reinforces or adds to change, rather than the desirability of the outcome. I will labor the point only because positive feedback is perhaps the most important element of the overconnectivity picture; it is a concept I will bring up throughout the rest of the book, so it makes sense to get well acquainted with it.

Feedback, whether positive or negative, occurs through a circular pathway called a loop. A signal travels from one source to another (A to B), then back again (B to A). Feedback loops can be longer—A to B, B to C, C to A, ad infinitum. As the loop gets longer and the connections get stronger and the number of loops increases, then the greater is the likelihood for creating large amounts of positive feedback. When a loop exists, information—or any other stimulus to an environment—can circle back to affect the originator of that stimulus: a comedian tells a risqué joke, and the audience laughs, signaling amusement; the comedian hears the laughter, becomes energized by the response, tells another, even more risqué joke, the audience laughs again, and a positive feedback loop is formed.

Negative feedback as engineers use the term is not about criticism; it is about stability. Negative feedback tends to moderate, even neutralize, change, keeping environments in balance. This is why engineers use negative feedback to control systems like the one that heats your house. If the house gets too cold, the system is out of balance, and the thermostat sends a signal ("Too cold!") to turn the furnace on. If the house gets too warm, the system is again out of balance, and the thermostat sends another signal ("Too hot!"), this time to turn the furnace off. In this manner, give or take a few degrees in either direction, the environment remains at the desired temperature.

Traditional market systems also use negative feedback to match supply to demand. When a commodity, such as copper, is in short supply, the market is out of balance and the price goes up. This price increase signals producers in the market to produce more. If the producers make too much, the price of the commodity falls. This drop signals the producers to cut back on production. This seesaw process ensures that supply usually matches demand.

Instead of bringing an environment back into balance, positive feedback reinforces and amplifies change, accelerating it rather than reining it in. When positive feedback is present—as is the case in many tightly interconnected environments—an initial stimulus works its way through the environment and back through feedback loops to provide more stimulus to the system. This reinforcement drives the system faster in the same direction and causes rapid change to occur. The more positive feedback that exists and the more feedback loops available to carry that feedback, the greater and more rapid the change: change creates more change, with increasing speed. In the home temperature control system example, positive feedback would have the thermostat's signal to the furnace be "Great heat; let's have some more," repeating it until the house became unbearably hot.

In the realm of global climate change, many experts are pointing to positive feedback as the reason for much of the accelerated change: increased carbon dioxide (CO_2) emissions lead to higher temperatures in the polar regions, which then lead to increased melting of polar ice and snow. The new melted surface of the Arctic sea ice, darker than the old frozen surface, absorbs more heat, which in turn causes still more warming—positive feedback at work

Most of us who have listened to anyone with a microphone and an amplifier have experienced an annoying by-product of positive feedback: the audio system stops amplifying the speaker's words and instead produces an ever-shriller, high-pitched shriek or low-pitched buzz, steadily increasing in volume until somebody turns down the volume or pulls the plug. When this happens, sound is bouncing off the walls and being fed back into the microphone. If the amplification is set just a little bit too high, say 10 percent, the system runs away and you hear an ear-shattering screech. With sound bouncing off the walls, getting amplified, and bouncing off the walls again, in no time at all the initial sound is amplified a thousandfold.

Acoustic engineers deal with this problem of too much gain in music venues by installing baffles that dampen the sound. If baffles have not been installed, someone turns down the amplification or pulls the plug. In social and economic systems we do the same type of thing to keep a system from running amok. In banking systems, the Federal Reserve establishes reserve requirements and sets discount rates in order to control the amount of feedback in the system.

In acoustic systems, 10 percent too much amplification can create a very unnerving noise, but 1 percent too much amplification can cause the same discomfort to your ears. It just takes a little longer for the positive feedback to create the screeching sound. When it comes to positive feedback processes, in some situations the Internet strengthens the positive feedback a little and in others a lot. And in still other situations the increased interconnections created by the Internet will actually create positive feedback where it had not existed before. When a lot of positive feedback kicks in via, say, e-mail and instant messages, things can become unpredictable very quickly. Teenagers, for instance, alert one another to an ongoing party in the neighborhood via Facebook and text messages. Word spreads like a brush fire among the kids, and within a few minutes dozens of young party animals descend on a classmate's house, taking many an unsuspecting parent by surprise.

A loop can exist with as few as two elements—a comedian and an audience—or as many as you can imagine, connected in labyrinthine ways. The only requirement, again, for these connections to constitute a loop is that one or more of the elements connect back to the originator of a given stimulus. A typical environment—say, for example, the economic environment of a medium-sized state—may have hundreds of loops connecting individuals, businesses, and government agencies in a wide variety of ways.

In situation after situation where large amounts of positive feedback are present, the path of least resistance is to go with the flow. It seems to be almost a rule of history that some form of vulnerability follows.

Positive feedback drives much of what we call progress. It helps give rise to the Silicon Valleys of the world, great cities like Chicago, and the world's powerful corporations. But it can also have an ultimately negative effect, as we'll see in the case of Pittsburgh, a perfect example of how an economic region succeeds through specialization driven by positive feedback, becomes locked in on that specialty, and then becomes vulnerable, and in the end struggles to survive.

In an economic context, positive feedback can cause success to build on prior success, and failure to create more failure, leading to collapse. If you create positive feedback in a stagnant economy by, say, lowering interest rates, you can encourage that economy to grow. If you create too much positive feedback with low interest rates, you can create financial bubbles and inflation.

Although this book is concerned primarily with the effects of positive feedback, the Internet can also be a key component in negative feedback processes and help to bring things under control. For example, when people talk about the role the Internet plays in bringing transparency to financial markets and thereby shining a spotlight on egregious incentive practices, they are talking about negative feedback processes facilitated by the Internet. Just as people use thermostats in their homes to prevent overheating, they are using the Internet to signal too much financial abuse, which in turn helps deter irresponsible behavior.

Most of the enthusiastic discussions about the role the Internet can play in encouraging more responsible behavior have focused on the negative feedback aspects of the Internet. But many of the proponents of this point of view have failed to comment on the role the Internet plays in positive feedback processes that drive overconnectivity.

THREE

How Overconnectivity Can Both Make Us and Break Us

ositive feedback can be good or bad. Frequently, we are only too happy to have it. Sometimes, we regret what it does. And we don't have to look very far back in history to see both its beneficial and its negative effects.

The story of Silicon Valley is a tale of positive feedback at its best. A slender, twenty-mile strip of land between Palo Alto and San Jose, California, the valley is a densely connected environment where geographic proximity, informal social networks, and the diffusion of knowledge from academic institutions all played an important role in the area's growth. And for the first forty years of its existence, Silicon Valley saw the far-reaching effects of positive feedback—long before the Internet.

It was at the start of those first 40 years that I first arrived at the place that would become Silicon Valley. In 1957, I had decided I would not merely save the country, but change the world while I was at it. I was a graduate student at Dartmouth College, seated in my electromagnetic theory class, when the professor, a dour man named Millett Morgan, announced that the Russians had just launched *Sputnik*, a 184-pound satellite orbiting the earth. *Vanguard*, our competing satellite, would not be launched for months and would weigh only about eight pounds. That seemed like a big problem to those of us sitting in the isolated hamlet of Hanover, New Hampshire. Professor

Morgan's tone was more somber than usual as he explained the difference in rocket power required to launch the heavier satellite, and the implications of that difference. The United States was hopelessly behind. Sitting in Professor Morgan's classroom that autumn morning, I decided there was little choice for me but to help the United States catch up.

That decision set the course of my professional life. It took me to southern California in 1958, to study electrical engineering at Caltech, and then to Stanford for my Ph.D. It led to my involvement in the computer industry and ultimately to Intel, where I spent much of my career. And it led, finally, to my decision to become a venture capitalist to help create companies that would help grow the economy and create jobs.

Silicon Valley as such did not exist then. Like much of California, agriculture was the principal industry in the thirteen-hundred-square-mile Santa Clara Valley south of San Francisco. Apricots were the main crop. As the writer Tom Wolfe once described it, acre by acre the fruit trees were uprooted and two-story flat-roofed office buildings with precast concrete walls went up. The state of California built a new freeway through the area, Route 280. Children of engineers began hearing the phrase "Silicon Valley" so often that they grew up thinking it was a name on the map.

Much of what made Silicon Valley an economic powerhouse began, of course, with the invention of the transistor, which was little more than three minute gold wires leading to a piece of processed germanium less than a sixteenth of an inch long, designed to alter and control the flow of electricity in circuits. Like the vacuum tube that came before it, the transistor could amplify a specific electrical signal, such as one produced by a radio wave. But the transistor did not require glass tubing, a vacuum, an anode, a grid, or a cathode. It drew a lot less current than vacuum tubes and got a lot less hot. Still better, transistors were a small fraction of the size of vacuum tubes and much more reliable. In fact, they could be made microscopic.

At the time, Silicon Valley was linked by social networks: friends and neighbors talking and meeting, people trading ideas generated at the local universities, engineers attending local technical society meetings, and firms doing business with one another, while learning in the process. These conventional forms of interconnection created the positive feedback loops that drove Silicon Valley.

Many venture capitalists established their businesses along Sand Hill Road in Menlo Park, a short drive from Stanford University and from the high-tech companies founded and run, in many cases, by Stanford alumni and professors. Over time, lawyers, accountants, investment bankers, recruiters, and consultants opened businesses in the area to support the high-tech boom. The top San Francisco law firms established offices nearby. Years later, the big New York investment banks did too. Then there were the informal social networks that sprang up. In the 1970s, there was the Homebrew Computer Club, where computer hobbyists such as Steve Jobs and Steve Wozniak, the founders of Apple Computer, went to talk about their inventions. The new Silicon Valley denizens lived for work. Highly disciplined, they put in long hours and kept working on weekends. And when they weren't working in the formal sense, they were attending technical society meetings. Or they were at Walker's Wagon Wheel, a watering hole behind a gas station in Mountain View. It was to the Wagon Wheel that members of the nascent semiconductor industry repaired on a regular basis to celebrate their successes, commiserate over a yield bust, swap ideas, or seek a job.

If ever I had a role model, it was Bob Noyce, who introduced me to Intel. Noyce was the coinventor of the integrated circuit. His 1959 invention had made it possible to put an entire electrical circuit on a chip of silicon smaller than the nail on your little finger. By 1964, the best engineers knew how to put ten circuits on a chip. And by the early 1970s, a thousand circuits could fit on a single chip. Year after year the figure kept rising.

It was people such as Noyce, and Gordon Moore, Andy Grove,

William Hewlett, and David Packard who proved to young engineers like me that if you could come up with a good idea and take good care of customers and employees, you could become wealthy beyond your wildest dreams. It didn't take long for venture capitalists to catch on to the idea that they too could prosper if they could find—and finance—the next Hewlett-Packard. As a result, by the late 1960s successes were beginning to emerge, creating the demand for still more venture capital and support services. The money supplied by a growing number of venture capital firms made it easier for entrepreneurs to obtain financing to start companies. Following on the heels of this success, investment banks specializing in taking high-tech companies public emerged.

When companies had successful initial public offerings, those employees with significant equity stakes suddenly became fantastically wealthy. And the beat went on. The enormous good fortune of a few companies created opportunities for a host of others. The success of Fairchild, Intel, and National Semiconductor, for example, created a demand for associated equipment. And soon dozens of other companies became part of the Valley's thriving ecosystem. Meanwhile, entrepreneurs continued to meet up with one another at technical society meetings, at events at their children's schools, or at the well-loved Wagon Wheel. Each meeting fed into the ongoing, steady stream of positive feedback processes.

When systems that perpetually produce creative ideas of great commercial value are mixed with ambitious and talented people in a free market economy, the systems are bound to be exploited—and exploited they were in the Valley. Venture capitalists and entrepreneurs ran thousands of entrepreneurial experiments. (My own firm, Mohr, Davidow, was one of the early venture capital firms to back semiconductor and software start-ups.) Many ideas got funded, many start-up companies failed or became what were known as the walking wounded (companies that lived on but had little future), and a few became great winners.

The success of Silicon Valley was driven by hundreds of positive feedback loops. The success of one company encouraged others, and their successes in turn encouraged entrepreneurs to create even more start-up companies. As these companies grew, they attracted venture capitalists, investment banks that specialized in start-ups, and teams of lawyers, bankers, consultants, and other professionals who helped the companies prosper and increased the likelihood of their success. Soon the universities, realizing that their graduates would make large contributions to the schools that trained them, began training more engineers and encouraging them to start companies. Wealthy entrepreneurs became interested in investing in and helping to create new companies. The result was more successes—positive feedback at its best.

Positive feedback is certainly not a new phenomenon. It has been with us since the dawn of civilization. More efficient sailing ships drove positive feedback in ancient times. Steam-powered vessels did the same for nineteenth-century trade. Railroads systems were one of the engines driving positive feedback in Britain during the Industrial Revolution and in the economic development of the United States, especially after telegraph lines were strung along the tracks.

The Internet had a similar effect on the physical communities that once defined Silicon Valley. The Internet today serves as a proxy for much of the Valley's physical networking. Instead of attending technical meetings, engineers subscribe to electronic mailing lists, read and write blogs, and network on LinkedIn. Instead of regular gatherings at the Wagon Wheel, which shut down in 1997, people shoot e-mails back and forth, between different office buildings on the same streets, between floors of the same office building, between cubicles on the same floor of the same office building. Of course, people still meet one another at their kids' soccer matches and at fund-raisers. But by and large, many of the physical communities that

once defined Silicon Valley have been replaced or dramatically augmented by virtual connections.

The rise of Microsoft, eBay, Google, Facebook, and Twitter was
driven by positive feedback. In the case of these companies, a positive feedback phenomenon called "network effects" was at work. The
term describes situations where the value of what one person does
increases the value to others for doing the same thing. Network effects
have been around for a long time. In the 1920s, when my mother was
a young girl in Reading, Pennsylvania, a number of different telephone companies competed for customers. But if you subscribed to
one, you were unable to talk with people using a different network.
As more and more people started using one network over others, however, it became vastly more convenient to use that network. The value
of being a customer of the leading network increased, and the value
of being a customer of a market laggard went down. This is what network effects are all about.

In the case of Microsoft, the more people who use its software,
the more valuable it is to be a Microsoft customer. If you are an individual, having knowledge of and experience with Microsoft products
means there are more places that will want to hire you. If you are
an employer, the more people there are with knowledge of Microsoft
products, the easier it will be to find trained employees. If you are
a customer, with so many other people using Word to create and
exchange documents, it is more valuable for you to use Word, so that's
what you do. Such network effects reinforced Microsoft's monopoly,
which grew so powerful that many of its customers became captive
to its whims.

Consider the Vista operating system, an updated version of
Windows that came out in 2005. For many customers, there was
little perceived advantage in Vista over the existing Windows XP but
when they bought new computers, they bought Vista along with it.

After months of being frustrated by the new system, many ended up reinstalling the old Windows XP. This then ran happily on their machines. But many are annoyed to have purchased Vista in the first place. They had found themselves in a classic position of vulnerability – victims of positive feedback and network effects.

Positive feedback can also play a major role in turning a mere happily interconnected city into a wide-reaching economic force. Pittsburgh is a perfect example of how an economic region succeeds through specialization driven by positive feedback, becomes locked in on that specialty, and then becomes vulnerable, in the end struggling to survive.

My father, Leonard Davidow, never attended high school. He was a book publisher in Chicago during the Depression, and his big break came when he realized that while people might not have much disposable income they now had plenty of time to read. He selected a few dozen classics, put rock-bottom prices on them, and sold thirty million copies in a single year. My father especially loved stories about successful businessmen, and one of his favorites was the tale of the rise of Andrew Carnegie, whose brilliant career paradoxically touches on a negative effect of positive feedback. In 1853, just before he turned eighteen, Carnegie became the private secretary and telegrapher to Tom Scott, the superintendent of the Pennsylvania Railroad's Western Division, based in Pittsburgh. In the next dozen years, Scott and other Pennsylvania executives noticed Carnegie's talent for business—and nurtured it. They favored young Carnegie with partnerships they hatched for bridge-building, iron-making, and constructing railroad cars. In 1865, at the ripe age of thirty, Carnegie announced his "retirement" from railroading and went into business for himself. The iron used by his ventures left much to be desired, however, and as the nation built railroads across the West, its price crept upward. One of his iron mills experimented with steel, a superior material, but found it difficult to make and prohibitive in cost.

On a trip to England in 1872, Carnegie toured the steel mills of Henry Bessemer, the inventor of a successful process for making inexpensive steel. Carnegie resolved to bet his future on steel, gradually winding up his existing iron, bridge and railroad activities. In 1875, Carnegie opened his first steelworks in Braddock, Pennsylvania, ten miles southeast of Pittsburgh. Carnegie named it the Edgar Thomson works for the Pennsylvania's legendary president. Known simply as the "ET works," Carnegie's plant became the most famous steel-rail mill in the world, and the site of innumerable experiments in hard-driving and high-output production. Convenient—and crucial—railroad connections brought in coal from southwest Pennsylvania and iron ore from the upper Midwest, and provided a means for shipping steel to eastern markets. Over the years, these and many other developments helped make steel rails the standard for the American railroad industry, driving the price of steel rails down from $160 a ton in the 1860s to $28 a ton in 1900. Along the way, Andrew Carnegie became the richest man in the world.

A combination of the railroads, western Pennsylvania's proximity to coal and iron ore, and the drive and ambition of men like Carnegie created a virtuous circle, where the success of one venture, person, or idea contributes to the success of another. Carnegie's career in the railroads gave him an understanding of the industry's needs while also providing him with a source for managers to run his steel mills. His relationship with railroad industry leaders provided insights that helped him design the right products for the market. Others, who developed low-cost methods for steelmaking and designed steelworks and steelmaking equipment, were also major contributors to the region's success. The growing prosperity of the railroads created demand for more steel, resulting in a prosperous steel industry that, in turn, created an ever-greater demand for iron ore and coal. The concentration of the steel industry in a single geographic region created opportunities to share technology and make the steelmaking process more efficient. Meanwhile, the interactions among inventors, coal and iron ore mining companies, the railroads, and the iron and steel manufacturers all contributed to making western Pennsylvania a leading steel center, with Pittsburgh at its heart.

Pittsburgh became highly connected. Carnegie had connections with the railroads, which in turn were needed to bring coal from the mines. An entire set of industries sprang up around the city as technology was developed to help build better steel plants. Pittsburgh became a nineteenth-century version of Silicon Valley.

The city's early success in steel—the result of historical chance and positive feedback processes generated through a web of interconnections, including geographical proximities, economic dependencies, and rapidly improving transportation and communication systems—led to specialization. Steel was the thing Pittsburgh did best, and, as such, the city lost many of the skills required to be competitive in other economic spheres. Pittsburgh had become locked in on steel. This wasn't necessarily a bad thing—at least for a while. Though focused on a single industry, the city's economy thrived. Jobs were abundant and innovation flourished. In the 1880s, local deposits of iron ore began to run out. New ones were discovered in northern Minnesota. After the Second World War, the industry began to ossify. It fell behind technologically, and relations with labor became hostile. In the 1970s and 1980s, U.S. steel producers came under increasing pressure from foreign manufacturers in Germany and Japan, which were using newer technology and had labor cost advantages. Then the Koreans, Indians, and Chinese entered the markets. As a result of global competition and mismanagement, Pittsburgh had lost its engine for growth, and the city entered a period of decline that took decades to reverse. By the year 2000, Pittsburgh's population was half what it had been in the 1950s. This story is an example of overspecialization, or what I have come to call a vulnerability sequence. Vulnerability can come out of nowhere.

Frequently in technology businesses a breakthrough will create a vulnerability. IBM, which specialized in mainframe computers (the hulking machines that for decades served as the underpinnings of corporate data processing departments), is a perfect example. When I first went to work in the computer industry for General Electric, IBM was dominant. One day I calculated that IBM was spending more on research and development for its mainframes than the General Electric Computer Department's total revenue. There was no conceivable way that anyone could ever unseat IBM, or so I thought. Then along came the invention of the integrated circuit; minicomputers soon followed, and less than twenty years later Intel invented the microprocessor. Suddenly mainframe computers were no longer as important. IBM's specialization in mainframes became its Achilles' heel.

In our overconnected world there will be more and more positive feedback that will drive us to specialize; we will become locked in and then vulnerable. Increased levels of connectivity created a prosperous Chicago with a fairly diverse and durable economy. The city did not become a victim of the vulnerability sequence. Pittsburgh wasn't so lucky.

Sources of vulnerability can surface in the most unlikely places. Consider the position Google now has in the computer industry. The company started with two Stanford graduate students noodling over new ways to search for information on the Internet. From that largely academic computer science problem emerged a company that now has Microsoft, and much of the rest of the computing industry, on the defensive. Whether Google too will someday find itself vulnerable to some innovation emerging from an unlikely quarter remains to be seen. But, given the complexity of Google's global reach and given what I now know about complexity and unpredictability, it would not surprise me.

FOUR

Expect More Accidents and Contagions

While studying complex systems, I thought back on Eugene Wigner's work, which suggested to me that big and complicated economic and social systems were vulnerable to big doses of positive feedback and unpredictability. When I mentioned this idea to a friend, he pointed me to a book written by Charles Perrow titled *Normal Accidents: Living with High-Risk Technologies*. The title seemed strange, because, like most people, I thought of accidents as being anything but normal. I considered them outliers, something we try to plan for and do our best to avoid.

Perrow, a renowned organizational theorist at Yale, claimed that in highly complex and tightly connected systems, accidents are a normal occurrence, and there is no way to avoid them. As a matter of fact, he went on to make an even more astounding claim: adding more safeguards frequently increases the probability that a horrible accident will occur. To prove his point, he described a number of catastrophic accidents—nuclear power plant meltdowns, petrochemical plant failures, and the collision of ships. Perrow argued that as long as systems don't become too complex, you can guard against single failures or surprising events. But once systems become highly interconnected, when multiple failures occur it is virtually impossible to avoid an accident or, in some cases, a disaster. Before long I was immersed in the study of accidents.

One of the most intriguing was the failure at Three Mile Island Nuclear Generating Station, near Harrisburg, Pennsylvania. In the end, the problem was traced to a relatively small water leak—perhaps no more than a few ounces. However, the multitude of interactions stemming from that cupful of water was breathtaking. The water seeping into the control system caused it to malfunction, which in turn made the reactor core overheat. At the same time, an operator error shut down the backup cooling system. At that point, a relief valve failed, draining more cooling water, triggering the partial meltdown. At this stage of the accident, there were forty people in the control room frantically trying to deal with the problems created by these independent failures and the unexpected results of their interaction. A number of audible alarms were sounding, and many of the control room's sixteen hundred control lights were flashing. Amid the chaos, plant operators took a series of desperate actions to prevent the core from further meltdown, although inadvertently many of those actions made the condition even worse by further reducing the flow of coolant water.

Finally, with the arrival of a new shift supervisor, the decision was made to override the system and the plant's standard operating procedure. This decision turned out to be right, and the general belief is that it averted the complete meltdown of the core and enabled operators eventually to bring the accident under control without any deaths or injuries to plant workers or members of the nearby community.

In the early 2000s, I gave several talks about the growing number of interconnections and the inevitability of accidents, and in some of those talks I speculated specifically on the problems the economy might encounter as a result of overconnectivity. I told my audiences that we had survived the Asian currency crisis of 1997 and the Russian financial crisis of 1998, but only barely. With a few more connections and interdependencies, those crises could have been far worse. Whenever I ventured into such territory, some people accused me of being a Cassandra. A former undersecretary of the Treasury told me my worries were misplaced. Economists told me I was being overly pessimistic, that tools were in place to cope with the scenarios I had projected. And for a while they had me convinced that they were right.

But as I watched the world grow even more tightly coupled, I started to worry again, feeling like a seismologist living in San Francisco who is certain there will be a major earthquake in the Bay Area eventually and therefore refuses to live in a seismically unsound house. Although I had less financial information than that hypothetical seismologist had geophysical data, I decided—even against the counsel of a financial adviser who for years had been urging me to be more aggressive—to move into a safer house, figuratively speaking, by lightening up my financial risk. Perrow's work had not merely captivated me; it was now influencing my investment strategy.

Because Perrow wrote his book on accidents in 1984, he unsurprisingly made no mention of the Internet. Shortly after the stock market melted down in late 2008 I sent him an e-mail, learned that he was wintering at Stanford, made a lunch date with him, and sent him an early draft of this book. Perrow is well into his eighties, but hale and hardy and still pondering problems of complexity and connectedness. As soon as we had ordered our food, he pulled from his pocket two pages of reactions to what I had sent him.

"I think you're on to something that isn't captured by traditional accident theory," he said. "As complexity theories and chaos theories and network analysis were evolving, they were not considering the hyperconnectivity issue." He was especially taken with my observation that had the Internet existed when past financial catastrophes occurred, those disasters would have been far worse.

After I explained more of my ideas, he asked, "Is the problem really about the connectivity or about the absence of control rods, so to speak—the lack of regulation?" He continued, "And is it really that everything is interconnected or that the rate of change is accelerating? I suspect that if governments could respond faster, the interconnectedness would not be as critical. So the problem may be lack of regulation in the market, not the connectivity." I said I had to agree.

We moved on to the concept of positive feedback, and Perrow reiterated that it isn't merely connectivity that the Internet enables, but also the compression of time. I chimed in that compressed time in turn creates still more powerful positive feedback loops, making predictions difficult and behavior fickle, while increasing the possibility of unexpected interactions. His vigorous nodding told me I had found a sympathetic ear.

We were working on our salad when he seemed to change the subject and asked, as we all sometimes do, about the role of moral authority in restraining a person from doing wrong. That is, how much do people rely on the physical proximity of others to influence their ethical behavior? We agreed that if some sense of collective vigilance influences our behavior, whether it be financial or physical—some awareness of physical community that makes us to do right or wrong—then the sense of anonymity accompanying most Internet-based transactions can skew our behavior to a potentially dangerous point.

After that lunch, I was more certain than ever about the Internet's role in creating accidents. And I was equally as confident as ever in the potential of dampers, baffles, and other safety measures to help keep situations from spinning out of control.

However, as Perrow himself has warned, some safeguards against accidents can end up making ultimate disasters even worse. Call it the Katrina effect: small fixes of big problems frequently contribute to still bigger ones.

New Orleans was founded in 1718 by French settlers on the Mississippi River. Within months the river overflowed and flooded the town, leading the residents to conclude that they had to control the water by building embankments, or levees. By 1724 the levees were three feet high. Still, the town flooded—in 1735 and again in 1785. By 1812, levees had been extended to more than 150 miles upriver, mostly to protect plantation lands. In the disastrous year of

1850, hundreds died when 32 levees were breached. Then, in 1882, 280 levees were breached, and many more hundreds died. The flood was the most destructive of the nineteenth century. Then, in 1927, a flood covered more than thirty thousand square miles of towns and farms, killing more than two hundred people in the process.

Each flood that occurred over the years prompted the city to raise the height of the levees and extend their length. Such action made New Orleans appear safe for more people to move there. And move there they did. By 2000, the population had risen to 484,000. The levees seemed to have confined the river and kept it from spreading over surrounding lands. But since the confinement narrowed the river, the flood crests were inevitably higher. So, perversely, the levees created the need for still higher levees. Yet the levees remained poorly designed, as did evacuation plans. On August 29, 2005, when Hurricane Katrina made landfall, it did more than $80 billion in damage and killed nearly two thousand people. Obviously, the increased population lured to New Orleans by the seeming effectiveness of the levees made many more people vulnerable to the catastrophe.

In sum, Katrina drove home the lesson that while short-term fixes have the attraction of seeming affordable and practical, they often mask problems that in the long run inevitably lead to greater losses.

The problems facing New Orleans run on a geologic clock; they can be measured in centuries. In an Internet-driven environment, change occurs at hyperspeed. As a result, problems pile up more quickly and accidents that should never happen end up happening frequently. Thus, in an Internet-driven environment we should be on the lookout for Katrina effects.

This same hyperspeed applies to contagions. When accidents happen they can frequently trigger contagions, which in turn require high levels of connectivity to sustain themselves.

Contagions are nothing new; we have lived with them for thousands of years, although we associate them most frequently with biological events. They require two now-familiar conditions in order to spread—interconnections and positive feedback. One sick person has to come in contact with another or pass the germs or virus along in some way. When one person infects many in a single act, such as sneezing in a crowded place, the likelihood of rapid dissemination increases. That is where the positive feedback loop comes in, since those sick people are likely to infect many more.

When levels of interconnectivity were low, contagions tended to remain localized. For example, the epidemics referred to by Hippocrates that coursed through Thasos in the late fifth century BC remained relatively contained because Thasos was an island. But by the Middle Ages, what with increases in trade and travel by sea, epidemics began to extend well beyond local boundaries. By the four-teenth century, advances in interconnectivity coupled with the pro-liferation of carrier types such as rats and fleas led to the spread of bubonic plague throughout Europe, killing a third of the population over a five-year period.

More recently, the influenza pandemic of 1918—which probably had its roots in Kansas and in the spring of that year was carried by American soldiers to the battlefields of France—quickly spread around the world to claim the lives of as many as forty million people in less than a year. Compared with the bubonic plague, the 1918 epidemic killed more people in much less time. This was due in large part to a denser world population, as well as the faster means of trans-portation linking cities, nations, and continents. Again, the main villain was connectivity.

However, my focus in this book will be on other types of contagions—economic, thought, and electronic. We are all familiar with economic ones—tulip mania in the 1630s, the South Sea bubble in 1720, the Great Crash of 1929, the Internet bubble of the late 1990s, and the 2008 global meltdown, to name but the best known. Economic contagions are always accompanied by thought contagions, the irrational greed that drives prices up and the panic and fear pro-ducing the opposite reaction.

We have come to talk about contagions with terms such as "self-fulfilling prophecies," "tipping points," "bubbles," "business tornadoes," "panics," and "crazes." People tend to liken them to the biological variety, but to do so is not quite accurate, and it is important to understand the differences.

Biological contagions are an absolute phenomenon in the sense that you either have the disease or not, and they are spread by physical contact. You can, of course, do some things to make yourself less susceptible, such as washing your hands frequently and keeping your immune system healthy. But when all is said and done, most people are either resistant to a disease or not. Few of us ever aspire to become infected with a disease in order to spread it. And carriers of biological contagions are usually victims themselves.

By contrast, with economic contagions the carrier of the "disease" often profits from its spread. For instance, short sellers in a bear market frequently start rumors and make dire forecasts in the hope of driving prices down. When they do so they are powering the positive feedback loops that drive the market's decline. Unlike the case of biological contagions, the psychological component of thought contagions means that people can be infected in a greater variety of ways. If someone sees investors lined up outside the bank next door, he is more likely to believe a rumor about his own bank and contribute to a full-blown market panic, but he can also ignore what he has seen, depending on his character, or worry to varying degrees.

Thought contagions can lead to momentous events, like bank runs, or trivial fads as benign as the hula hoop craze. As well as negative and trivial effects, they can have very positive ones, such as the monumental worldwide humanitarian effort that greeted the news of the tsunami that killed more than three hundred thousand people in December 2004. Even isolation-minded Americans who ordinarily wouldn't have donated money any farther afield than their local Boy Scout troop were moved. By the time the contagion had run its course, charities around the U.S. had raised nearly $2 billion in aid.

The Internet was deeply involved in spreading that thought contagion, just as it has thousands of others. Numerous blogs provide anyone who possesses a modicum of computer literacy with a low-cost means of spreading ideas, recruiting new members, pumping stock prices up, and driving them down. To repeat, thought contagions have a huge psychological component, whereas the physical basis of biological contagions makes people's levels of susceptibility absolute.

Electronic contagions are something else entirely. Because computer viruses; worms, and other forms of electronic scourges are endemic to the Internet, they require no physical contact between people in order to spread. A virus can burrow into a computer, pick off your e-mail address book, and spread to everyone you know without anyone even being aware of it. What happens in your computer can infect that of a friend on the other side of the world whom you haven't seen or talked to in years.

Contagions of all kinds need networks. A harbinger of what can happen in networked environments occurred in 1987, when the stock market collapsed. That crash turned out to be a perfect example of a series of accidents or unexpected events at work in a highly connected, complex environment triggering a financial contagion. Powered by computer-driven trading, it ran its course in just a few days' time and affected markets around the world, though particularly in the U.S. And it happened, as so many crashes do, in the midst of a sustained economic boom.

In the five years prior to 1987, the Dow Jones Industrial Average (DJIA) had more than tripled. Of course, one could argue that a correction was in order. But that would ignore the many positive economic factors that had driven the market's growth over the prior half decade—good corporate earnings, a business-friendly administration that had promoted generous corporate tax benefits, low inflation and tax rates, tax incentives, and stock retirements from mergers—all factors that traditionally inspire confidence among economic forecasters.

Then, just as Charles Perrow would have predicted, a number of "accidents" or unexpected events occurred in a tightly connected environment, and financial disaster ensued. In four trading days, between Wednesday, October 14, and Monday, October 19, the U.S. market lost about 25 percent of its value. Here's how it happened: on the morning of October 14, the federal government announced a higher-than-expected trade deficit of $15.7 billion. This was unexpected event number one. It drove the dollar lower, raised fears of inflation, and for the first time in several years pushed the thirty-year Treasury-bond yield above the psychologically significant level of 10 percent. Unexpected event number two: later that day, Congress announced that it was seriously considering eliminating tax benefits that occurred during corporate turnovers. Unexpected event three: this announcement raised concerns that takeovers would become less attractive and subsequently lower the demand for stocks.

The initial impact of these events was small, with the market declining only about 1 percent in the hours immediately following the announcements. But as prices fell, a phenomenon relatively new to the market kicked in—in the form of a safeguard called "portfolio insurance." This risk management tool, intended to minimize an investor's loss in the event of a market meltdown, would have made little difference under normal circumstances. But when prices started to fall, computer programs automatically shifted clients out of stocks, and the fact that a large number of major investors were employing this same strategy (a new form of interconnection) further drove what was well on its way to becoming a full-blown contagion.

Over the next two days, both the stock market and the futures market were in turmoil. On Thursday, October 15, the DJIA fell 53 points, causing portfolio insurers to become even more active, and the next day the DJIA dropped 108 points. But this was just a minor precursor to what would happen when the market opened the following Monday. Over the weekend, an enormous overhang of sell orders had built up, as managers of "insured" portfolios were dumping their stock. On Monday morning, waves of selling by these managers hit the U.S. markets. By the end of the day, the DJIA had dropped by 503 points, or 23 percent, and the Standard & Poor's index had dropped 29 percent. The fact that the equities market couldn't withstand the waves of selling generated by portfolio insurers serves to reinforce Perrow's point that a would-be safeguard can become the problem itself.

The effects of the 1987 crash were felt around the world. A relatively small group of portfolio insurers drove the contagion. Primitive computerized trading systems intensified it. One can only imagine what would have happened if the Internet had been widely available. Had more computers been tied to the network and been using algorithms to trade more portfolios, had e-mail and instant messaging existed, had market news been instantaneously accessible, had rumors circulated around the globe as quickly as they would twenty years later, then the 1987 crash might have happened in a few hours instead of a few days and been far more severe.

Just as the telegraph made rail connections more effective, the Internet is making our current forms of physical connectivity more powerful and effective. It has become the nerve system of the information-driven society of the twenty-first century, carrying the freight in a frictionless manner, at virtually zero cost. It is tying together systems that were once disjointed, and increasing the correlation between them. It is creating a world with much more positive feedback, one that is more accident-prone, volatile, and susceptible to contagions.

We must learn to adapt. Most of our institutions were designed for lower levels of connectivity. A lot of adjustments will be needed to accommodate the new environment. True, no silver bullet exists. But much can be done to facilitate adjustment. Details will be discussed in the final chapter, but many of the ideas proposed will be based on the need to reduce the amount of positive feedback in the system or, to put it another way, reduce the gain in the system by weakening or even breaking interconnections.

The 2008 global economic meltdown was a financial twister so destructive it made everyone wonder where it came from. The answer, I insist, is a densely woven thicket of conduits and networks called the Internet. Conceived in the relatively placid world of academic research, this invention three decades later has revealed its unintended consequences, prompted by positive feedback, contagions, vulnerabilities, and accidents. The Internet is the ultimate self-fulfilling prophecy: it has made itself great, and by doing so it has become a catalyst in an overconnected world.

FIVE

The Ghost in Our Midst

Ask people what they think qualifies as the most significant milestone in the evolution of the Internet, and the answers are certain to vary. Some would say it was reached in 1989, when the first commercial services started to emerge. Others would argue that it was the first mass spam, in 1993. Still others would take the question, turn it into something very personal, and say it was without a doubt the first time they saw a "page" on the World Wide Web.

I believe that the most overlooked event in the growth of the network occurred early one autumn evening in 1988, when a brilliant, introverted Cornell University computer science graduate student named Robert Morris typed a few commands into a campus computer, hit return, and went out to dinner. Morris had just launched what he intended as a harmless experiment: a computer program whose sole purpose was to slowly copy itself from computer to computer around the Arpanet, the Internet's precursor. The idea was to have one copy of the program live secretly in each computer it invaded.

It would be hours, Morris figured, before he would see any results. He had planned to go home after eating, but his curiosity got the better of him; he couldn't resist returning to campus to see how his little program was progressing. But when he sat down at his computer, he couldn't log in. To his horror, he found that the program had reproduced itself with such unanticipated swiftness that computers all over the network—which linked thousands of military, corporate, and university computers around the nation, including those at Cornell—had become jammed.

As it turned out, in the time it took Morris to put on his jacket and walk out the door, the program had already been spreading. Within a few minutes, it was fanning out over the entire network, and computers were infecting one another as toddlers do in a day-care center. Within a few hours, thousands of computers had been clogged to the point of being unusable. So complete was the infiltration that the electronic virus had come full circle and choked Morris's own computer.

Morris had made a simple calculation error that caused the program to copy itself hundreds of times in every computer it reached rather than infecting each machine just once. When he realized his mistake, he was mortified. The Morris worm, as it came to be called, became front-page news. Morris was eventually convicted of a felony and sentenced to four hundred hours of community service.

For years he was unable to shake his reputation as the kid who took down the Internet. Finally, enough time passed, and he and a friend started a company, which they eventually sold for tens of millions of dollars. Today Robert Morris is a professor of computer science at M.I.T.—and something of a folk hero. Many computer security experts have argued that the famous mishap was an important and useful demonstration of the potential vulnerability of computers.

Young Mr. Morris imparted his valuable lesson to us more than two decades ago, and the incident remains one of the best illustrations of how a tightly coupled system such as the Internet can lead to an accident of disastrous proportions. It was with that one extraordinary act that the nation was made aware of a new ghost in our midst. However, although it opened our eyes to how interconnected the network was, it should also have made us see how interconnected the network would become. When Morris released his worm, the machines affected were, for the most part, at universities and government research labs. Monetary losses were calculated in terms of work hours lost. Six thousand of sixty thousand host computers on the network were penetrated. That's 10 percent. And the only reason more weren't infected was that the program was instructed to target just a certain subset of computers. Now let's think about what would happen if Morris did the same thing today. With nearly six-hundred-million hosts (that's one for every ten souls on the planet), a modern Morris worm that hit 62.5 million computers would be taking down entire corporate Web sites, banking systems, and airline reservation sites. All of Google's thousands of computers in Mountain View, California, could freeze up.

When Morris launched his worm, I thought about one of my favorite historical figures—Head-On Joe Connolly. Beginning in 1896, Head-On Joe, a native son of Iowa, produced a series of "cornfield meets" in which trains crashed head-on. Over a period of thirty-six years, he staged seventy-three of these spectaculars, involving 146 locomotives, many with old wooden coaches that burst into flames when pots of blazing charcoal ignited gasoline-soaked interiors. Tens of thousands of spectators paid a dollar or more to watch the behemoths collide at full speed.

Unfortunately, these mock accidents reflected a reality. Railroads in the United States at the time were cheaply constructed and poorly maintained. Sharp curves, steep, bumpy grades, water-logged and termite-invested trestles, and inadequately ballasted ties all combined to create a fertile environment for accidents. In 1890 alone, thousands of people were killed and many more injured in train-related accidents. The government regulated the railroads to make them safer, but accidents continue to happen. And although those accidents are disturbing, we have come to accept them as part of living in a complex world. Robert Morris's stunt, whose consequences were truly accidental, made me think about Head-On Joe because Connolly made intentional sport of unreliable railroads, just as many people who spread computer viruses today are often simply strutting their stuff.

I say the Morris worm still qualifies as the crucial event in the Internet's history to date because of yet another analogy to Head-On Joe. Here we have an electronic railroad—I would even venture to call it the most important connection system in the history of humanity—carrying hundreds of tons of vital virtual freight every day, when in fact it wasn't designed to do any such thing, lacking as it did much security and including so few mechanisms for checks and balances. Then along comes one young smart aleck and demonstrates, by launching a clever but flawed piece of software, just how highly connected and vulnerable that electronic railroad is. But instead of heeding its warning, we've built an unfathomably huge number of vital enterprises on top of a densely connected and highly unreliable foundation. And although cars are required to have bumpers, roads have speed limits, and trucks have restrictions on where they travel, to this day the Internet remains unregulated and unmanaged. Why do we accept this? And how did we get here?

If ever there was a humble beginning, it was the Internet's. It got its start as four nodes on the Arpanet, a government-financed experiment in computer networking for universities and military sites. And it was born of simple frustration. In 1966, a man named Bob Taylor—the director of the Information Processing Techniques Office at the Pentagon's Advanced Research Projects Agency—found himself confounded by the fact that he had three different computer terminals in his office that couldn't communicate with one another. He went into his boss's office and twenty minutes later had a commitment for $1 million to start an academic research project in computer networking.

The aim of the network Taylor had in mind was modest in ambition and narrow in scope. The idea was to allow far-flung computer scientists and engineers working on U.S. military contracts to share expensive computing resources. By 1968, the network existed as a series of doodles on a few 8.5- x 11-inch sheets of paper. The doodler in question was Larry Roberts, a computer scientist from M.I.T. whom

Taylor had recruited to Washington for the job of designing the network. In his drawings, he imagined many configurations: one drawing was shaped like a star, with each point comprising a single node; another looked like a wagon wheel; still others were dense labyrinths. In the end, he settled on a network shaped like a spider's web. In technical terms, this type of configuration is known as a distributed network, meaning—you guessed it—that there is no central computer, no central cop directing traffic. The main point of this design is to achieve a high level of redundancy, so that if trouble occurs anywhere, the network will route around the problem. It's a simple yet ingenious notion, and, as it turned out, only something so highly distributed could grow into the ubiquitous network we know today.

For the actual transmission of information, Roberts decided on a scheme called packet switching: each message would be split into uniform "packets," with an address on each one, then sent off on its journey through the network. The packets would be sent in the right general direction, choosing the best path available at that moment. The individual packets making up a single message might end up taking different routes, only to be reassembled into readable form upon their arrival. Roberts was doing his work in parallel with another scientist named Paul Baran, an engineer at the Rand Corporation who had developed an interest in the survivability of communications systems under nuclear attack. Baran's network was distributed like Roberts's, and it called for a high level of redundancy.

Little did Larry Roberts and Paul Baran know that they were creating something that would someday extend far beyond its intended realm. Roberts in particular enjoyed scientific puzzles, and to him working out the configuration for an efficient data network was simply an interesting intellectual challenge. The last thing he was thinking of was online banking—and certainly not virtual dating. Nor was he thinking for a millisecond about the critical foundation he was laying for what would become, years later, the strange economics of cyberspace.

In 1995, Chris Anderson, a writer for *The Economist* who went on to become editor of *Wired* magazine, pointed out how one of the many remarkable things about the Internet is that once you have paid your monthly connection charge of, say, $49.95 to Comcast, as far as you can tell, that's it. Send one e-mail message or ten thousand, and the price is the same. In fact, each e-mail message does cost somebody something because it consumes a tiny bit of "bandwidth," the transmission capacity of the expensive data pipes making up the Internet. But Internet providers have no way of billing for such tiny bits of usage, so they multiply the number of their subscribers by the average network usage to calculate the capacity they need to lease, which gives them a fair idea what to charge. As long as the average usage doesn't change much, this plan works, for, although the Internet runs on telephone lines, it uses them much more sparingly than voice calls do. This is because of the "bursty" nature of data communications.

When the Arpanet came into existence, all communications networks were "circuit-switched," which meant that a communications line was reserved for one call at a time and held open for the duration of that session. Back then, voice calls were analog signals that needed a lot of electronic space to avoid interference, so a single call took up an entire line for the duration of the call. A phone call between two teenage girls would tie up a line for as long as the girls commiserated over their boyfriends. By contrast, information flowing over data networks is digital and split up into packets, which do not need a line to themselves. Thus, when you send a message on the Internet, you are sharing a plentiful and cheap resource—the entire bandwidth on the line.

Roberts, of course, had no reason to ponder the implications of his creation. That is, he had no reason to take into account the fact that transmitting data so reliably, efficiently, and inexpensively would someday give rise to spam and computer viruses. He had no idea that a couple of decades down the road it would cost the same to send an e-mail message around the world as to send it to the person seated in an adjacent cubicle. In fact, he had no idea what e-mail was, because it hadn't yet been invented.

By 1971, the number of nodes on the Arpanet had increased to fifteen. Most were on university campuses, with a few at government-funded research labs. A few years later, as other data networks began to emerge, it became clear that intranetwork communications weren't sufficient. There was a need to allow different computer networks to talk to one another, using an internetworking protocol.

Here is where things started to get really interesting. The most important development of all came in 1973, with the creation of the Transmission Control Protocol and Internet Protocol, or TCP/IP, the basic set of data communications rules by which the Internet now operates. The design of that protocol fell to two young computer scientists named Vinton G. Cerf and Robert Kahn. That summer, the two men hunkered down in a conference room of a hotel in Palo Alto, California, where they wrote, sketched, and argued, all the while passing a yellow legal pad back and forth to capture ideas as they came. Two days later, the two scientists knew they had the makings of a solid technical paper. What they did not know was that they had created the essential underpinnings of the Internet, giving the network its power and reach for decades to come.

In 1974, Cerf and Kahn published their paper, "A Protocol for Packet Network Intercommunication," which created the structure for TCP/IP. The Kahn-Cerf Transmission Control Protocol defined a standard way to package chunks of data into "datagrams" for sending across the network. The Internet Protocol then provided a standard way of putting those datagrams into envelopes addressed to any computer in the world. Like postal sorters, the computers along the way could look at the addresses on the envelopes to relay them to their destinations without needing to look inside the envelopes.

The secret of TCP/IP was breathtakingly simple: think up a way for networks to share data that will work with any kind of network, of any size, carrying any kind of information, on any sort of machine.

Let anyone use it, for free, with no restrictions or limitations. Then just stand back.

Today, TCP/IP is embedded in everything from laptop computers to telephones to televisions. It's like the railroad that carried the Sears catalogs to customers a century ago. And Sears, the retail store, was an application that rode the rails. Even proprietary networks using different data standards can be part of the Internet as long as they package their data to the TCP/IP standard when they meet one another. But increasingly they use TCP/IP internally, too, because otherwise they miss out on the thousands of Internet software programs. These programs allow the Internet to be used for applications its founders never imagined, from telephone calls to live rock concerts. The fact that TCP/IP is an open standard means more users speak a common language and reach a potentially huge audience.

Even after the Internet supplanted the Arpanet in the 1970s, the network remained the province of computer scientists, physicists, biologists, and other researchers at a few dozen universities around the country. For years the Internet consisted of just a few hundred host computers, almost exclusively in American military labs and academic computer science departments. But the word was getting out to other academics. And from very early on, there were signs that the network was used less for conducting network research than for communicating, pure and simple. In 1979, a trio of graduate students started a group of newsgroups they called Usenet. Users from around the world joined the discussion groups to talk about politics, religion, and thousands of other subjects. The Internet was on its way to becoming a mass communications medium.

By 1980, people were beginning to buy home computers. In 1981, *Time* magazine named the computer its Man of the Year. In January 1984, Apple announced the Macintosh. Its user-friendly interface swelled the ranks of new computer users. And the writer William Gibson published a novel called *Neuromancer,* in which he coined the term "cyberspace," calling computer networks a "mass consensual hallucination." Also in 1984, the Internet grew to the point where extensions to addresses became necessary, and the domain name system was developed—".gov" for government agencies, for example, and ".edu" for educational institutions. Hosts in other countries took a two-letter domain indicating the country.

Well into the 1980s, to be on the growing Internet was to be among an elite. The Internet was a private playground—and an expensive one. Only those institutions with government funding could join the club, and maintaining a university's annual connection cost upward of $100,000. Using the network was still difficult and frustrating, but its power was already obvious. No other method to hook up universities around the world was so universal and so flexible. Internet users invented ways for many people to participate in open discussions, created software and document libraries on the network, and made them accessible to all. This was exciting stuff for computer scientists and some other academics, but it remained a cloistered world.

E-mail would change all that. The Arpanet was not intended as a message system. In the minds of its inventors, the network was intended for resource sharing, period. But the human desire for communication was too strong a force to resist the promise of electronic mail.

As cultural artifacts go, e-mail belongs in a category somewhere between found art and lucky accidents. That is, there was no grand vision for an earth-circling message-handling system, but by virtue of the Internet's geographic reach, e-mail was transformed from an interesting toy into a useful tool. And once the first few dozen nodes were installed on the Arpanet, early users found themselves using it for decidedly unscientific correspondence.

The big rise in e-mail traffic became the largest early force in the network's growth. E-mail would become the long-playing record of cyberspace. Just as the LP was invented for connoisseurs and audiophiles but spawned an entire industry, electronic mail grew first among the elite group of scientists on the Arpanet, then later spread across the entire Internet. By 1990, the Net had grown to more than three hundred thousand hosts. That year, Argentina went online, as did Austria, Belgium, Brazil, Chile, Greece, India, Ireland, South Korea, Spain, and Switzerland. And two years later, the number of computers connected to the Internet surpassed a million.

As it turned out, we hadn't seen anything yet, because this was all before the World Wide Web had been introduced to the world at large. In the 1980s, an Oxford-trained computer scientist named Tim Berners-Lee was beginning to think about ways to approach documents the way the brain works—associatively. He began writing programs based on his ideas, and he based those programs on hypertext, a nonsequential layering of information whereby words and phrases in a document can be highlighted to let readers skip from one source to another rather than read in a traditional linear fashion. Part of his idea was to turn those documents into pages, giving each an address by which it could be referenced. For the name of the system itself, Berners-Lee toyed with a few ideas. First came Mine of Information, or MOI, which he decided seemed too egocentric. Then came The Information Mine, or TIM, which was even worse. Finally, he settled on World Wide Web.

By Christmas Day 1990, the first Web server (a computer that holds Web pages) was up and running on Berners-Lee's own desktop. He also wrote the original browser, a program for gaining access to and reading information on the system. Using the HTTP protocol, computer scientists around the world began making the Internet easier to navigate by inventing point-and-click browsers. One browser in particular, called Mosaic, created in 1993 at the University of Illinois, would help popularize the Web, and therefore the Net, as no software tool had yet done.

With the World Wide Web in place, the Internet was suddenly more accessible than ever before. Instead of typing in strings of commands, people could now navigate their way around cyberspace by simply clicking on images and words. And this point was key. Without the Web, it would not have been feasible to create virtual facsimiles of the artifacts of everyday life. Online banking would not have become popular, to say nothing of virtual shopping at Amazon.com and eBay.

Remember that overconnectivity occurs when institutions change so quickly that the environment in which they are embedded is unable to cope. Or the reverse happens: with the increase in interconnections, the environment changes so dramatically that the institutions become overwhelmed by cultural lag and are unable to cope. The focus of this book is interconnectivity driven by the Internet, but there is little doubt that due to the rapid advances in data communications and transportation some more limited level of overconnectivity would have inflicted itself on society even if the Internet had never been invented.

The brilliant, flexible, and scalable design of the Internet has created the ghost in our midst. Internetworking, a technology created to enable scientists to share computing resources on computers operating on different networks, created a foundation for a deep stack of applications that would affect almost every aspect of our lives. First it was e-mail. Then it was the World Wide Web, powered by browsers and hypertext. Then came search. With these tools in place, almost any activity we engaged in could be powered by the Internet—local commerce, world trade, government, financial transactions, shopping, social networking, identity theft, music, news, movies, gaming, terrorism, and so forth.

Suddenly the ghost was everywhere. And wherever it went, it frequently brought with it positive feedback that drove change at startling rates—change that enveloped environments and institutions to a degree we barely understand.

SIX

Why the Internet Is Accident-Prone

By 1995, the masses started arriving, well, en masse. Web traffic doubled every couple of months, resembling biological growth, like algal bloom or guppy reproduction. It was clear by then that the Internet had become a commercial enterprise. And evidence of this was beginning to show up everywhere. Under the stale ham sandwiches in snack boxes, airline passengers found floppy disks for signing up with AOL. Home-grown Internet service providers and online bulletin boards with cute names like backfence.net were popping up all over. But perhaps the most telling sign that the Internet had reached the point of no return—that it was destined to become an entrepreneurial Wild West—came in 1993, when Martha Siegel and Laurence Canter, a pair of immigration lawyers in Arizona, sent out what is thought to be the first mass spam.

One day, a Usenet regular in a discussion group about food logged in and instead of recipes and restaurant critiques found an offer for legal services from Siegel and Canter. Believing the lawyers had sent the e-mail to the food group in error, he e-mailed them in return. "This has nothing at all to do with food," he wrote. "Please be more polite in the future and keep announcements in relevant and appropriate groups." He received the following in response: "People in your group are interested. Why do you wish to deprive them of what they consider to be important information?"

The startled food lover later wrote that he had "expected that the author would recognize that he had done something incorrect once it was pointed out to him. Gosh, was I wrong!"

Internet purists were incensed and demanded that the spammers recant. But the two lawyers merely dug in their heels. The incident came to be known as the "Green Card Spam," and, as it turned out, Siegel and Canter were in the vanguard of a big trend. Within two years, newsgroups all over cyberspace were clogged with spam, and electronic junk mail was showing up in e-mail in-boxes everywhere. And although the Green Card incident occurred nearly two decades ago now, little progress in stemming the tide of e-mail spam has occurred since then.

At home, PCs had made computing power affordable, and modems had allowed them to be connected over telephone lines to commercial "online" services and "bulletin boards," or electronic discussion groups and software libraries set up usually by enthusiasts. Both of these grew steadily, but not explosively. Each had disadvantages. The networks offered by CompuServe, the leading online service provider, and others that followed in its wake were national, even global, but they were closed systems. The providers controlled what was available. Private bulletin board systems, which had sprung up in the thousands, were unrestricted but usually confined to a small group of users in geographic proximity to the host computer.

For the Internet's first twenty-five years, the U.S. government ran parts of it, funded network research, and in some cases paid companies to build custom equipment to run the network. But as the Internet's operation was transferred to private carriers throughout the 1990s, and as the network began to serve as a connection point for commercial networks, most of the government's control evaporated.

Also in the mid-1990s, a handful of doomsayers predicted that the Internet would melt down under the strain of increased volume. They proved to be false prophets, yet the Internet's creators, for all their genius, failed to see what the network would become once it left the confines of the university and entered the free market. By 2005, there was no doubt that the Internet had evolved into an information utility as ubiquitous and accessible as electricity.

Today, the Internet operates with surprisingly few hiccups twenty-four hours a day—and with few visible signs of who is responsible for keeping it that way. There are no vans with Internet Inc. logos at the roadside, no workers wearing Cyberspace hard hats hovering over manholes. This is yet another of the Internet's glorious mysteries. No one really owns the network, which is now a sprawling collection of networks owned by various telecommunications carriers. The network depends on the cooperation and mutual interests of the telecommunications companies. Those so-called backbone providers adhere to what are known as peering arrangements, which are essentially agreements to exchange traffic at no charge.

The Internet is the steam engine of information efficiency. And its freight is an amazing collection of stock trades, e-mail, video, and retail transactions carried by high-speed, low-cost data communications systems, all using TCP/IP. Global financial markets use TCP/IP, enabling currency transactions of some \$3 trillion every day. The Internet applications we all know and love—Google, Yahoo!, Facebook, and Twitter—depend on it. Even Web browsers like Firefox and Safari are, in the end, merely applications that rely on TCP/IP as their foundation. It is the global adoption of TCP/IP over the years that gave the network its reach and power. And it is that very reach and power that have allowed the Internet to become not merely massive, but extremely vulnerable.

In 1973, Vint Cerf and Bob Kahn had no way of knowing how ubiquitous TCP/IP would one day be. Nor did they foresee how vulnerable society would become as a result of that ubiquity. Similarly, as Bill Gates watched his Windows operating system grow into the computer industry's dominant software, he little knew how fragile that would make us. Standardizing one set of protocols—or one piece of software so that it becomes entrenched in governments and the military, in global corporations, telephone networks, utility and transportation systems, and hundreds of millions of homes—creates an environment in which malicious acts have the potential to cause massive economic and physical damage to systems of vital importance to our society and the world. Such standardization means that one malicious piece of software can be created and distributed worldwide at relatively low cost, providing terrorists and criminals with inexpensive weapons of mass social destruction. Well-designed attacks have the potential to bring down power networks, shut down financial systems, disable transportation systems, and much more.

Pundits have long warned of cyberwarfare, and recent events have lent legitimacy to those concerns. In early 2007, questions were raised about Russia's involvement in the problems of one of the most wired countries in Europe, Estonia, when it experienced a month-long interference with its networks. Government communications failed, banks came under siege, and ATMs stopped working. In 2009 reports circulated that spies from Russia and China had attempted to map the American power infrastructure. Software fragments had been left behind that could be used to destroy system components.

Positive feedback drove our standardization on the Internet, as well as the specialization on a few technological options. The subsequent lock-in on those options has created the Mother of All Vulnerability Sequences—something the inventors of the Internet could never have imagined. How were they to have foreseen hackers or spies disabling the Internet and taking down our power systems, financial structures, and phone networks? How were they to anticipate the computer viruses, spam, and cyberattacks of the late twentieth and early twenty-first centuries, menaces they had unwittingly enabled?

As I studied how highly connected states shift to overconnected ones, I realized that atomic energy provides a pretty good analogy.

Nuclear reactors start off underconnected. In a nuclear reactor, neutrons collide with uranium atoms and split them in the process we know as fission. When fission occurs, the atoms give off other neutrons. As you pull control rods out, the reactor goes "critical" and generates a lot of heat, which can be used to create steam to drive turbines, which in turn generate electricity. But if the control rods are not positioned correctly and get pulled out too far, too much heat is generated, and the reactor goes into what nuclear engineers call thermal runaway. The situation can get out of control in a few thousandths of a second, so quickly that it may be physically impossible to reinsert the control rods and stop the reactor from melting down. Thermal runaway does not cause a nuclear explosion but can lead to fires and conventional explosions that spread radioactive materials. This is what happened in 1986 at the Chernobyl plant in the Soviet Union. Nuclear weapons, on the other hand, use critical reactions to create nuclear explosions.

As I looked at the 2008 economic crash, at what the Internet has done to privacy, and at e-mail spam, I found that things had become overconnected but that the control rods were nowhere in sight. The environments in cyberspace had gone from a highly connected state to an overconnected one of thermal runaway, so to speak. And in those circumstances where something analogous to control rods did exist, things had gone so out of control that the tools that were supposed to deal with the situation were no longer capable of doing so.

Take the 2008 financial crisis as an example. For years the control rods had been pulled out too far, metaphorically speaking—in this case, interest rates and risk premiums, the excess rates charged for risky investments, both of which had been set too low. Once the highly connected economic system became overconnected and went into the economic version of thermal runaway, the old control techniques no longer worked. The result was an economic meltdown. Merely cutting interest rates could not restore the economy. Suddenly the government found itself bailing out banks, purchasing toxic assets, and trying to save the auto industry.

Our social and economic environments are composed of those things with which we interact. If we abruptly increase the number of connections and change the things with which we interact, then we abruptly change the environment, sometimes with disastrous consequences. When individuals, governments, businesses, and economic and social institutions experience this type of abrupt environmental change, they reach a "critical" state. They become overconnected.

In the fall of 2008, Iceland's three biggest banks failed. The value of its currency fell by 75 percent. The country's citizens took to the streets. These were the symptoms of a state that had undergone abrupt change to its social and economic environment. Iceland's newly transformed financial system was on the brink of extinction.

How did this happen? How did an island in the middle of nowhere, a country known best for its salt cod industry, with a gross domestic product of about $10 billion in 2003 (about 10 percent of IBM's annual revenues), become a banking epicenter with assets many times the size of its economy? What enabled the Icelandic banks to support prodigious borrowing and lending binges? How did this tiny country see that engorged banking industry go to ruin within two weeks? How, in the course of just three years, did two online banks end up saddling their nation with a total debt equal to about one-third of the country's domestic output? And how did the ailing economy of plucky little Iceland come to serve as an object lesson for the financial pain circling the globe?

In October 2008, when news of the Iceland catastrophe began to spread, the press had a lot to say about the symptoms but very little to say about the underlying cause. Riveting stories were told of failing banks, street riots, bankrupt consumers, and the disastrous free fall of the krona, the Icelandic currency. But those are all symptoms. To speak of them is roughly akin to a doctor examining patients complaining of pain, swollen glands, and a fever, and then diagnosing their illness as pain, swollen glands, and a fever.

What was the underlying cause of Iceland's symptoms? How does a small country that has for centuries functioned so well independently suddenly find itself on the brink of total collapse? Let's look at the details of this remarkable story.

SEVEN

From Fishing to Finance

The remote and rugged island of Iceland started out toward a state of overconnection in 1994 with the injection of a free market ethos into what had long been a largely nationalized economy. Then the coming of the Internet supercharged those changes, and everything accelerated. Transactions that might have taken a few days and a modicum of forethought now took a few minutes, and soon Iceland was ensnared in a web of interconnections, thereby embedded in a new environment for which elected officials, regulators, and citizens were completely unprepared. A nation skilled in fishing was no longer attempting to net cod in the treacherous North Atlantic. It was now betting its future on big catches in the volatile world of high finance.

In hindsight, something was terribly wrong from day one. This was a country of roughly three hundred thousand people (a little larger than the population of Anchorage, Alaska, or Stockton, California), without an iota of experience in the realm of international finance. The cast of characters in control included a former mayor turned prime minister, a grocer, and entrepreneurs with holdings in the prepared-food business. As finance replaced fishing as the new "it" industry in Iceland, MBA programs filled up with young upstarts who previously might have studied to become sea captains at the Icelandic School of Navigation. Many Icelanders now seemed to look at the financial success that Wall Street could yield and say to themselves, "How hard can that be?!" Yet they drove Iceland into a toxic, overconnected state, putting on the world stage a band of amateur players backed by a stage crew of politicians and regulators who cheered on the irresponsible behavior.

For centuries, Icelanders had lived in relative isolation—that is, the country was underconnected. The size of its institutions—banks, regulatory agencies, and government departments—was limited by the sparse population and the lack of engagement with the outside world. But as interconnectivity increased—a great deal of it driven by the Internet—the market for Iceland's overly generous banking services expanded to the rest of the world. Without those connections, Iceland's banks wouldn't have grown so aggressively. Catastrophe would never have happened. In a sense, however, it was inevitable, because embedded in Iceland's history of isolation was a desire to become more connected to the world.

A hundred years ago, Iceland was the poorest nation in Europe. For centuries, it coped with isolation and harsh living conditions. Eking out a living on the edge of the inhabitable world was a constant struggle. Two pandemics in the fifteenth century wiped out sizable portions of the population. In the late eighteenth century, a volcanic eruption devastated the country, and the ensuing toxic fallout killed approximately half of Iceland's livestock, resulting in a famine that wiped out about a quarter of the population. Just getting anywhere from Iceland was difficult enough. And in the winter, getting anywhere within Iceland was even harder. Although the country was remote and few people traveled, merchant ships sailed to and from the island.

In spite of these difficulties, Iceland had strong ties to the other Nordic countries, as some of the early Vikings sailed to Norway to seek positions as court "skalds," personal poets and storytellers to the kings. Later, in the nineteenth century, elite Icelanders traveled to Denmark to study.

For centuries, however, Iceland was a peasant colony, as colonialists, first from Norway, then Denmark, oppressed the population. The Danish king forbade Icelanders to own ships, and they were not permitted to trade with anyone save traders who had purchased licenses from the king. Usually what was brought to Iceland was rotten food, flour filled with worms, and other goods sold at exorbitant prices that the population had no choice but to buy. All of this, coupled with famine and a harsh climate, weakened the nation greatly. Still, miraculously enough, the people retained a strong spirit. It took tremendous fortitude just to survive.

Alda Sigmundsdóttir ("daughter of Sigmundur") is a journalist with a popular blog called icelandweatherreport.com. She has been translating into English a collection of century-old letters exchanged among her relatives, an extraordinary fact in itself, considering the rugged terrain that mail couriers at the start of the twentieth century had to travel by horseback or on foot. The letters convey a strong sense of what life was like at the time, painting a bleak yet oddly inspiring picture. Alda's great-grandparents lived on a farm with their four children. Her great-grandfather was a fisherman on a small vessel. If the weather changed suddenly—and it frequently did just that—he and his companions found themselves in a dire situation far out at sea. Many drowned, including Alda's great-grandfather. Few knew how to swim, and even those who did could not survive long in the Arctic temperatures. Although formal education was offered by and large only by teachers who traveled the country and lodged at farms for limited periods, most people were able to read and write. In fact, like their ancestors before them, Icelanders in the early twentieth century placed a premium on education. People saved their money to pay for it, and despite a life of hardship and poverty, the nation was always literate.

Nearly a century later, Icelanders were among the first on the planet to get wired. Consider Iceland's cultural focus on education combined with the nation's general enthusiasm for novelty, and it's easy to understand why. Surrounded by the stormy ocean and frustrated by years of separation, Icelanders were natural candidates for embracing something like the Internet. Indeed, Iceland had always responded to its geographic and linguistic isolation by finding ways to communicate with the outside world, whether that meant learning foreign languages, forming a steamship company, founding an airline, or rapidly implementing an electronic infrastructure that would connect it to the world as never before.

As happened in many places, the Internet arrived in Iceland via a university. In the summer of 1989, the country got its first direct Internet connection, linking the University of Iceland in Reykjavík with a network based in Denmark called NORDUnet. That was routine enough. But three years earlier something far less routine had already happened. In 1986, Pétur Thorsteinsson, a schoolmaster at a primary school in Kópasker, a swatch of a village in the northeast, grew curious enough about the Internet to go out in search of a way onto this emerging information thoroughfare. But there was no AOL or EarthLink, or if there was, getting on from Iceland was close to impossible. It took Pétur four years, but by the end of that interval he had set up an educational network, with three towns linked by dedicated high-speed lines to one another and to the country's Internet backbone. By 1993, nearly 80 percent of Iceland's primary schools were connected to the network, along with three-quarters of the country's secondary schools. At first, teachers were reluctant to adopt the new medium, which was used mostly for e-mail. But they eventually made computer communication a part of their everyday lives.

It seems a fair guess that when Icelanders embraced the Internet, they viewed it as a solution to the isolation problem that had long defined their country. The instant door to the outside world must have seemed a revelation.

By 1999, nearly 60 percent of Iceland's population had Internet access from home. By 2008, the percentage had risen to 99, with only the most marginalized of citizens left out. Iceland was set to build on the policy changes and reforms that had recently been introduced.

The worldwide rise of the Internet coincided almost magically with economic reforms in Iceland. And the man instrumental in bringing about those changes was Davíd Oddsson, a charismatic politician with an incisive mind and sharp wit. Oddsson ("son of Oddur") had been a producer of radio comedy shows, holds a law degree from the University of Iceland, and was elected mayor of Reykjavík at the age of thirty-five. He went on to become Iceland's longest-serving prime minister, from 1991 to 2004. Oddsson represented the right-of-center Independence Party. He was fond of quoting Milton Friedman, the famous University of Chicago laissez-faire economist, and one of his political role models was Britain's Margaret Thatcher.

With Oddsson in charge, privatization proceeded at a brisk pace. The corporate tax rate was lowered from 45 percent to 18 percent. In 1994, Iceland joined a newly established free-trade zone called the European Economic Area (EEA). Icelandic citizens were now free to work in other EEA countries, and Icelandic enterprises were permitted to operate there. And in line with Oddsson's overall plan for reform, many businesses were privatized, from telephone companies to fish-processing plants and, most important, the banks.

Prior to these reforms, Iceland had been in a moderately connected state. The citizens were comfortable. After the reforms, Iceland shifted to a highly connected state. Many positive feedback loops were created. Change was about to occur at a very rapid rate. By 2003, the country's two largest banks—Landsbanki and Kaupthing—had been sold to the private sector. But here's the strange part: the new investors seemed to have little actual experience in banking. The largest share in Landsbanki—a whopping 45 percent—was now held by investors who had made their money operating a brewery in Russia. Kaupthing was sold to two brothers who had become wealthy in the prepared-food business in the U.K. Those two banks began to focus on investment banking along with their commercial banking activities, with the accompanying high-risk. The new owners seemed to be using the banks to fund their own private ventures, in Iceland and, increasingly, abroad. And the third-largest bank, Glitnir, which had been created a few years earlier through the merger of several other banks, had also started to place increasing emphasis on investment banking.

In their new, highly connected state, the banks forged strong links to global financial markets and, with help from the Internet, found new and easy ways to finance their ventures. Suddenly all of Iceland was awash in cheap capital, which had been efficiently transported to its door through the World Wide Web. Unfortunately, those at the helm did not seem to be aware of the inherent dangers.

Among them was Prime Minister Oddsson himself. Oddsson's formal training was in law, but that didn't stop him from taking the helm of one of the country's most important financial institutions. After stepping down as prime minister in 2004, he was appointed as chairman of the board of governors of the Central Bank. This, it turned out, was not a prudent move. Oddsson might have been able to do the job if Iceland had remained in an interconnected state, but not in a highly connected environment.

Still, in spite of the banks' problematic ownership and equally iffy stewardship, privatization injected them with a new sense of purpose. But there was a problem: together, the three banks had assets of only a few billion dollars, a fraction of Iceland's entire gross domestic product. Glitnir, Landsbanki, and Kaupthing were about the size of large community banks in the U.S. that focus mostly on local markets. (To put it in perspective, consider that Community Trust Bank, which serves just the state of Louisiana, is a billion-dollar bank.)

Banking is a sophisticated business, but the basics are pretty simple. Banks make money by first collecting deposits, for which they pay modest amounts of interest. The banks then turn around and lend the money out at higher interest rates. The federal government insures single accounts for up to $250,000. The government also regulates the amount of capital banks must have on hand, as well as their loan-to-deposit ratios. It also inspects the quality of the assets on the banks' balance sheets. Under normal circumstances, this oversight ensures that banks will be able to pay depositors and meet their commitments to lenders. This degree of regulation in turn engenders trust among depositors willing to lend the banks money at low interest rates in return for keeping their savings safe.

In 2007, just one year before the financial crisis, Moody's, which rates the creditworthiness of corporate borrowers, made lending money to Iceland's banks very attractive by giving them its highest possible rating, AAA. Moody's pointed out that there had been "no bank defaults in the last 30 to 40 years in countries with a history of supporting banks." Moody's went on to argue that Iceland would always have access to capital and that Iceland's banks, each of which accounted for more than 25 percent of the financial system, were too big to fail. But these explanations failed to convince the critics, and within days of defending the upgrade Moody's dropped its ratings by three notches.

Where things get tricky is that the money banks lend is often out for long periods—in thirty-year mortgages, for example. On the other hand, deposits and money lent *to* banks are shorter-term propositions. In the case of deposits, customers can withdraw their money from the bank at any time. Banks depend on being able to keep borrowing and collecting new deposits to replace the accounts that leave.

A big problem occurs when large numbers of loans to the bank don't get renewed or when large groups of depositors and institutions all demand their money back at the same time—an event known as a run on the bank. In order to return the money to depositors and people who have lent them money, the banks have to get back the money they have lent out. They have to call in the loans or wait until they mature. In times of crisis, they can't get enough money back fast enough. When this happens the banks go broke.

The three Icelandic banks pursued foreign business with a vengeance. Glitnir, Landsbanki, and Kaupthing offered lending and other banking services to foreign clients that included companies in the seafood, retail, pharmaceutical, air transport, and telecommunications industries. With cheap credit readily available, the banks borrowed heavily abroad, reinvesting the funds in both domestic companies and abroad—frequently companies that were closely tied up with the shareholders of the bank or its favored clients. The Baugur Group, for example, whose owners had a large stake in Glitnir, built a retail empire in the U.K. and Denmark with the backing of Iceland's banks, with chains that included the department store House of Fraser and Hamleys toy stores, and established Danish department stores, such as Magasin du Nord and Illum. The owners of Landsbanki snapped up a telecommunications company and pharmaceutical company in Bulgaria, and Kaupthing's owners, through investment companies, acquired a major stake in one of the largest insurance companies in the Nordic region, among other investments.

Kaupthing, Glitnir, and Landsbanki did their investing initially by borrowing money from loan syndicates. They also issued bonds denominated in foreign currencies, and they engaged in the so-called carry trade, whereby a financial institution borrows funds in markets with low interest rates and relends in a market with high interest rates. As it happened, Iceland's Central Bank had raised interest rates sharply a few years earlier in an effort to cool down the Icelandic economy, and by June 2007 interest rates in Iceland were a whopping 13.3 percent, making the country an attractive prospect for speculators. As a result, Iceland's banks were becoming increasingly dependent on hot money—money that flowed into Iceland to take advantage of the high interest rate but that would quickly flee the country at the slightest hint of trouble.

The high interest rates attracted foreign investment, which created a demand for kronur. This demand drove up the value of the currency by more than 50 percent between 2001 and 2005. So, if you were a hedge fund looking to generate big returns for your investors, you borrowed lots of yen and other currencies where the interest rates were low at the time and bought kronur. Here is the beauty of the process. You and other hedge funds created a self-fulfilling prophecy—a type of positive feedback loop. If you were paying 3 percent on your loans in yen and collecting 13 percent on your loans to borrowers in kronur, you were making 10 percent on the spread. But things got even better: when you and your hedge fund brethren piled into the krona market, you created demand for kronur that drove up the value of the currency. Now your investment might be making 15 percent. Of course, others would find out what you were doing and make the same investment, creating even more demand for kronur and keeping the process going.

The key to making money in these situations is being agile—getting in quickly when things are going up and getting out fast before things collapse. Whether individuals are trading currencies, making investments, or just paying debts, they are always searching for better and faster ways to transfer money. History provides lots of examples.

In 45 BC, Cicero used the equivalent of a bill of exchange to pay for his son Marcus's education in Athens. Cicero's friend Atticus was owed money by Xeno, an Epicurean who lived in Athens. It was agreed that Xeno would pay off his debt to Atticus by paying for Marcus's education. Cicero would then reimburse Atticus. The whole point of this convoluted exercise was to avoid the risky business of transferring actual coins from Rome to Athens.

It is believed that Arab traders invented bills of exchange in the eighth century and that the Lombards and the Jews brought this method of monetary transfer into general use. In the fourteenth century, Italian bankers used the bills to transfer money to the Levant to support the Crusades. In 1307, the king of England, Edward I, used bills of exchange instead of coins and bullion to transfer money collected for the pope. Today, London still bears the mark of these methods. Lombard Street in the City of London runs through a piece of land granted to the goldsmiths from Lombardy by Edward I, and until the 1980s it was the location for the head offices of most U.K.-based banks. What ancient and medieval bankers had discovered was that it was easier, faster, and safer to send a message than to send coin or bullion.

As recently as the middle of the twentieth century, moving money was difficult, slow, and cumbersome. When my father went to Europe on business, he carried a letter of credit with him. When he needed cash, he went to a bank that he knew would honor the letter. The bank officials would enter the transaction on the back of the letter in order to ensure that my father did not exceed the limit. But wait! It gets even better. The bank that issued the letter of credit would charge a fee for the service and place a hold on the money in the account while the letter of credit was outstanding, which gave them the use of the money in my father's account. It was all very quaint, and time-consuming, and, of course, very profitable for the bank.

Bits flowing over communication networks have since replaced checks and paper documents. And the key event in international electronic funds transfer took place with the birth in Brussels in 1973 of the Society for Worldwide Interbank Financial Telecommunication. In 1977 SWIFT went live, and in its first year of operation the network transmitted ten million messages. A SWIFT message could consist of the communication leading up to a funds transfer, the transaction itself, or the acknowledgment of the transfer. By 2003, SWIFT was handling two billion messages annually, and in 2004, after years of operating over a private network, SWIFT migrated to the Internet. The move expanded the availability of SWIFT, increased its capacity, and further enhanced efficiency while reducing the cost of transactions. Progress at SWIFT was ideally timed to support the expansion of banking in Iceland. The vacuum cleaner found it easier to keep sucking in the money. SWIFT also made it easier to pull money out of the system when investors got spooked.

Whether or not Iceland's bankers understood the impact of money with electronic wings is not clear. Unfortunately, but perhaps not surprisingly, they were paying little attention to recent history—very recent history, in fact. Had they looked over their shoulders, they would have seen the country's future. In 1997, the Asian currency crisis had threatened the world's financial system. Iceland's strategy bore an eerie resemblance to the ones used by Thailand, Malaysia, Indonesia, and the Philippines. When international lenders refused to renew short-term high-interest loans when they matured, the value of the currencies collapsed, Thailand's by as much as 42 percent. Of course, Iceland was different. In just a few years, its sky-high currency would fall by 75 percent.

When environments change dramatically, the people most deeply immersed in those environments often do not see, understand, or react to the change. A big shift occurred when Iceland joined the European Economic Area, giving its banks the freedom to set up shop anywhere within the European Union. The only stipulation was that they had to have a deposit-insurance fund in place in the home country, to compensate depositors up to a minimum stipulated amount in the unlikely event of a bank collapse.

The EEA agreement enabled Iceland's banks to be integrated into the European Union. Oddsson's reforms freed them from restrictions and enabled them to pursue the opportunity aggressively. But the agreement was deeply flawed. It's self-evident that a country with such a small population would also have a small deposit-insurance fund—a fund not nearly large enough to cover deposits that a bank may collect from residents in other European Union states. So the Internet had allowed the Icelandic banks to suck up deposits from around Europe, but without safeguards in place to prevent a calamity. The EEA agreement went into effect in 1994, before the Internet began its global domination.

In other words, the regulatory system had not kept pace with the advancement of connectivity. It remained static and incapable of curtailing irresponsible behavior on the part of the banks. In this situation, positive feedback could run wild. Iceland would have shifted to an overconnected state even if the Internet had never been invented. But the Internet accelerated the process.

In fact, how a small country in the middle of a big ocean could have become a banking giant *without* the Internet is hard to see. SWIFT expedited the flow of money. The Internet facilitated the traditional banking business by making it easier to communicate and exchange long documents and coordinate the activities of people spread across geographies. So the Internet increased the level of positive feedback in the system and made the crisis bigger. It also delivered the coup de grace: it enabled the creation of online banks.

In spite of numerous assurances by Oddsson and other banking officials, the depositors in Iceland's banks were effectively uninsured. To make matters worse, the banks embarked on a strategy that set them up for a classic credit squeeze. If the people who supplied them with cheap credit suddenly wanted their money back, the banks did not have it to return. It was tied up in longer-term loans and investments, including loans made to the shareholders of the banks themselves. The key to avoiding the meltdown was to keep the money flowing in.

But things were starting to unwind. In March 2006, the Danske Bank of Denmark issued a report noting that Iceland's external debt was now 300 percent of gross domestic product (GDP). (By comparison, the external debt of the United States is about 100 percent of GDP.) It forecast a dramatic fall in the value of the krona. Icelanders reacted with anger to the report from their former colonial rulers. The research department at Glitnir said that "the Danske Bank report looks written with the intent of putting the Icelandic economy in the most unfavourable light possible." KB-Bank (Kaupthing) issued a special rebuttal that said the Danske Bank "report has numerous factual errors and is fraught with inaccurate and wrong use of Icelandic economic data."

Accurate or not, the report did not escape attention. In April 2006, the major rating agencies began to downgrade their assessment of Iceland, citing concerns about the banks. Investors panicked, and both the currency and the stock market plunged 25 percent within a week. Soon lenders to the banks began to demand a premium for making loans. It became too expensive for the banks to finance themselves in this fashion. They had to find a cheaper way.

Inside Icelandic banking circles, the impulse was to dismiss such concerns. But sophisticated investors had begun to pull their deposits out of the banks, and the search was on for new ways to raise cash. The answer seemed clear: find more depositors who would be sufficiently attracted by high interest rates that they would overlook the risks that might be involved. On October 10, 2006, Landsbanki announced the creation of a new online savings bank—a logical move, since Iceland had been one of the first countries in the world to introduce online banking. The new banking unit was called Icesave; it offered banking services in the United Kingdom, and it existed only in cyberspace. Some twelve months later, Kaupthing followed suit with the launch of its Europe-wide online banking unit, Kaupthing Edge, and a short while after, Glitnir joined the fray with the online bank Save&Save—although it would hardly get started before being thwarted by the Icelandic bank collapse a few months later.

The plan, for all intents and purposes, was a fine one. By the time Icesave was rolled out, people all over Europe were already accustomed to online banking, and Icelanders were no exception. And, although the bankers themselves weren't savvy when it came to international finance, they knew that a virtual bank could be built quickly and cheaply in cyberspace, because in cyberspace real estate is cheap and your potential customer base is vast. All that was required was a little software, high-interest rates, and credibility.

EIGHT

How the Internet Tricked Iceland

When I was growing up near Chicago, my friends and I often took the electric train to the movie theater in nearby Glencoe to catch a Saturday matinee. On the way from the train station to the theater, we walked by the imposing façade of the Glencoe National Bank, a victim of the Depression. Still empty in the 1940s, the building served as an ever-present reminder of past excesses.

In the 1950s, backed by my father and other local businessmen, the bank reopened. I would frequently accompany my parents there, and whenever they needed access to their safe-deposit box, I got to see the bank's massive, awe-inspiring steel vault. I remember the imposing façade, the sense of stability and fiscal security it inspired, and the fact that it "belonged" to the community. It was a local institution made even more local by the restrictive covenants written into the Illinois constitution that prohibited branch banking, which in turn ensured that a banker looked the customer in the eye, knew firsthand about that customer's trustworthiness, and stood by the bank's word.

Standing in front of that bank summoned to my mind a vision of the U.S. Capitol, or the even more august Supreme Court building. Like thousands of others, for years I have judged books by their covers, movies by their titles, doctors by the diplomas on their walls, people by their clothes, and banks by their buildings. Sure, I dig a lot more deeply, but first impressions do count.

Today, however, I often no longer have the option of seeing or touching something physical when making my decision whether to trust an institution. When I think of the Glencoe National Bank building, it seems completely out of place in the virtual world where I now dwell. And the very idea of a local bank seems so 1950s. I want my bank to travel with me on the Internet and on the ATM card in my wallet. The concrete building front has been replaced by the pixel façade of a Web page. The wait in line for a bank teller has been replaced by the instant it takes for a page on the Internet to refresh itself. The intelligence of the person helping me has been replaced by clever software. I now find myself judging an institution by its Web site. In short, what were once the Corinthian pillars of business are now trustworthy home pages.

I have asked myself why I feel so secure in my virtual relationships with the financial institutions I use. And I think back to the advice given by Ted Levitt, the Harvard marketing guru who counseled that when selling intangible products, tangible evidence is very important. In cyberspace, such tangible evidence starts off with a well-designed Web site that is easy to navigate. It makes you feel that the institution is solid and its employees smart. Of course, I also want to know that the vault is secure. So a tedious log-in procedure seems worthwhile. At one institution I first give my account name. Then I get back a picture of a specific animal I've selected so I know I am on the right site. I am then asked for my password. Sometimes I am asked questions about my first dog's name or my favorite color. All this makes me feel my money is safe in the vault. At institutions where the process is less complicated, I feel less secure.

Of course, the ultimate test of any banking institution is whether you can get your money out after you've put it in. In the case of those I deal with, wiring and transferring money online is a snap. I have instant access to records, allowing me to confirm that transactions have taken place, to check my accounts, and to see that the credits and debits have been made. I can even pull up images of both the front and the back of checks I've written.

When Iceland's banks decided to go in search of new customers, the U.K. turned out to be the perfect target. There, banking customers had dozens of online options from which to choose. Even supermarkets were offering high-interest-rate savings accounts. For those comfortable with the Internet, one virtual bank with a well-functioning Web site is as good as another, as long as it can be made to appear safe. A virtual bank can collect assets from anywhere in the world where it is legally entitled to operate. All it needs is a good Internet connection.

Initially, not much distinguished Icesave from all the other online banks. So Landsbanki hired a public relations firm based in the U.K., called Kinross + Render, to launch the brand, which it went about doing with gusto. One of its first moves was among its smartest. From the start, the firm sensed the need for a physical presence— what Ted Levitt called a "tangible clue"—to inspire people's trust. It organized one-on-one briefings with journalists, who were given goodie bags filled with coffee mugs, mouse pads, chocolates, and various trifles from Icelandic businesses. It sent reporters on junkets to Iceland itself. Key marketing concepts it crafted for Icesave were integrity, transparency, and, in a tip of the hat to the ancient Vikings, "managed aggression."

Kaupthing Edge employed a slightly different strategy. With a branding campaign run out of Iceland, Edge was marketed all over Europe. Its name was meant to suggest "cutting edge," and it was designed as an upmarket product for forward-thinking, Internet-savvy clients.

Both PR campaigns highlighted the many advantages of online banking. Customers could check their balances whenever they liked, see if checks had cleared, and confirm the status of transactions. They could transfer money easily, and watch the transmission happen almost in real time. All that transparency built trust, as did the fact that an online bank was accessible twenty-four hours a day. Both banks offered excellent log-in procedures. Possibly the greatest factor in creating trust in Icesave and Kaupthing Edge was that deposits were guaranteed under the Icelandic compensation scheme. In fact, when he was interviewed about Icesave on British television in 2008, Davíd Oddsson, the former prime minister and radio entertainer, blithely stated that all deposits in Icelandic bank branches were doubly secured with the sovereign guarantee that if Landsbanki declared bankruptcy (which seemed a very remote possibility at the time, at least to the public) the coverage of deposits "would not be too much for the state to swallow—if it would like to swallow it." Of course, the problem was that Icesave and Kaupthing Edge were being backed by a country that might simply be too small to do so.

Meanwhile, the PR machine continued to grind out promotions, and the media gushed approval. The new virtual banks became instant hits with the Internet literate, attracting depositors from all over Europe who were saving for houses, holidays, and retirement. It hardly hurt that Icesave's PR people also promised that the bank's interest rates would remain above the Bank of England's base rate for a specified period of time. The credibility of Icesave—and, by extension, Iceland—was crucial to the campaign. Many Europeans already knew Iceland's reputation as a hip and high-flying country. More than a few had vacationed there. Moreover, it was a West European nation with a strong democratic history. Had Icesave been created in, say, Bulgaria, it never would have had the credibility it needed to attract such throngs.

Within five months of its launch, Icesave had acquired more than 60,000 customers and deposits of some £2 billion. Within its first year it had gotten more than 40 percent of all new Internet deposits in the U.K., and by the time it celebrated its first birthday it had more than 110,000 customers on board and £4.4 billion in deposits. In a single year, Icesave had captured amounts equal to about one-quarter of Iceland's gross domestic product. Had a United States bank achieved the same relative size as Icesave, it would have had assets of close to $4 trillion, or double the assets of the largest

American bank. Icesave had achieved in one year what no U.S. bank had ever accomplished.

One of the most important numbers to consider when measuring a bank's health is the deposit-to-loan ratio. The higher the ratio, the better. A healthy deposit-to-loan ratio is around 1 to 1. That is, for every dollar held in deposits the bank lends $1. From 1998 to 2003, Icelandic banks were in a very strong position, with an average deposit-to-loan ratio of greater than 3 to 1.

But within a few years that changed, especially for Landsbanki, whose aggressive lending and borrowing caused the bank's deposit-to-loan ratio to fall below 0.4 to 1. The bank desperately needed new deposits. This is where Icesave came in. It was the ideal vehicle for collecting deposits to buoy Landsbanki's balance sheet. Icesave was so effective at gathering deposits that by mid-2007 Landsbanki's deposit-to-loan ratio had doubled to 0.7 to 1. Still, by most standards, that was dangerously low. In the United States in 2007, the average deposit-to-loan ratio for all banks was 1.1 to 1.

Buoyed by the success of Icesave, Kaupthing launched its Kaupthing Edge brand in Finland in October 2007 and would branch out to ten more countries before the collapse of the mother bank twelve months later. By the end of June 2008, Kaupthing Edge had collected a total of 3.1 billion euros in deposits and was on a roll. Kaupthing's goal was to have deposits account for 40 percent of all loans within twelve months of the launch; six months later it had already achieved that goal. The money poured in—and was used to finance high-risk loans, mostly to the owners of Kaupthing and their business associates.

Icesave and Kaupthing Edge were not limited to the U.K. In May 2008, Icesave launched in the Netherlands, collecting 1.7 billion euros in deposits in the five months before Landsbanki collapsed. At the time of the collapse there were plans for further expansion. One young banker told the journalist Alda Sigmundsdóttir that he was taken aback by the swiftness with which the online banks could work. "You could get money in just like that," he said, snapping his fingers.

There were some glitches that in hindsight should have given depositors reason for concern. Icesave's administrative systems were having trouble keeping up with the rapid pace of the overconnected environment. Icesave was reassuring customers that when they opened an account, their initial deposit was banked on the day of receipt, so they were receiving interest from day one. But some customers were sending in checks without writing an account reference number on them, making it difficult to credit their accounts. Also, anyone who went on the site with a query that required a human response had trouble getting one. E-mails started out by saying the wait for a response would be five days. That soon changed to ten days, which amounted to Pony Express response rates in the Internet world. Still, insisted Icesave officials, "We have not been overwhelmed."

Other glitches were slightly more alarming. In late August 2008, the Swiss media reported that an e-mail had been sent out to Swiss customers of Kaupthing Edge informing them of a new special offer. That was all well and good, except that the e-mail contained no text, simply a long list of e-mail addresses of the bank's clients. When pressed for comment, the bank acknowledged that a "technical problem" had caused the erroneous e-mail to be sent. The glitch reportedly caused some serious tensions between Kaupthing and the Swiss banking regulatory agency. In the end, Kaupthing was let off the hook with strict orders to ensure that a similar violation would not happen again.

So here is what happens when all you have to do is walk across your living room, turn on your computer, fill out an online form or two, and click *submit*: before you know it, you are in possession of a savings account earning more than 5 percent interest, and no matter where you and the bank actually are, your money is growing. And when hundreds of thousands of people do the same thing, something huge happens.

In just a few years, an entirely new way of economic life had been introduced into Iceland's relatively stable, all-but-socialist society. By 2006, the average Icelandic family was three times as wealthy as it had been in 2003—and far deeper in debt. Indeed, the economy was growing at a rate of more than 5 percent a year, far faster than that of most of Iceland's trading partners. By 2005, Iceland had become, on a per capita basis, the world's fifth-richest country.

The high level of connectivity was having no small effect on the lives of Iceland's citizens. Soon after the Iceland meltdown in October 2008, an article appeared in *The Wall Street Journal* with the headline "As Banking 'Fairy Tale' Ends, Iceland Looks Back to the Sea." It told the story of Kristján Davídsson, a fisherman-turned-banker. Six months later, I set out to learn from the aforementioned Alda Sigmundsdóttir a little bit more about Kristján and how he was faring.

As it turns out, it doesn't take long for Icelanders, once they meet one another, to establish someone they know in common. This was the case with Alda and Kristján (Icelanders also usually always refer to one another by their first names). Kristján, it turned out, was the brother of one of Alda's close friends. He is from a small town called Thingeyri on Iceland's West Fjords (on the head of the beast that Iceland looks like when you view the country on a map). Kristján's father was a fisherman, and Kristján grew up working in the industry. As a child, his dream was to attend the College of Navigation in Reykjavík and become a trawler captain, but he got distracted by fisheries science and ended up doing a bachelor's degree. He worked for various companies in the seafood sector before founding his own consulting company, taking on projects related to fishing. Eventually he got bored working on his own and put the word out that he was looking for a job. In 2001 he was summoned to Glitnir Bank for a meeting. The bank was looking to enter foreign markets and planned to focus on the fishing industry, among other sectors. Despite his lack of banking experience, Kristján was offered a job. The bank didn't need any more bankers—they had enough. What they needed were fisheries experts. The offer appealed to Kristján because he wanted to learn something new. He'd been considering entering an MBA program but knew that by joining the bank he'd learn all he needed to about finance. For him, it was just like going back to school, only he was getting about a 10 to 15 percent increase over his salary as a freelance consultant. He decided it was a great idea, a way to learn about finance from the inside out.

The bank's "We don't need bankers" attitude is a perfect example of overconnection at work. The Icelandic banks had become tightly connected to a new environment they did not fully understand—the world of international finance. They didn't "need bankers" because they thought they had lots of them. In reality, they didn't need fishermen and were in desperate need of bankers. But on one point Kristján was absolutely correct: he was about to learn about high finance from the inside out.

Kristján's stint at the bank turned out to be a roaring success. He and his group carefully chose the countries they wanted to operate in and offered their services to a subset of companies. The group did extremely well, the seafood industry was on a roll, and Glitnir Bank quickly became a name in the global finance industry.

The Internet played an important role in Glitnir's success. In overheated financial markets, speed is of the essence. The market is competitive, and executives' reactions are frequently driven by emotion—the desire to win and capture the prize. The Internet allowed Kristján and his colleagues to run documents back and forth instantly for editing and tweaking—a process that just two decades earlier would have been vastly more time consuming and difficult, requiring the use of mail, faxes, and couriers.

Kristján and others like him instantly became role models for young people infected with the mania, who were flocking to universities to study finance. Glitnir and similar institutions aggressively recruited the most talented of these young Icelanders. Every year, Glitnir would invite the top graduates from the business, engineering, and computer science departments at the University of Iceland and Reykjavík University for a lavish dinner featuring seductive presentations about the bank and its work. Glitnir skimmed the cream from the top.

Stories abounded of talented people from just about every commercial sector being summoned to meetings at the banks, wooed over lavish lunches or dinners, and made offers that they couldn't refuse. Alda, too, became the target of the headhunters for the banks, who wanted to hire her as a translator. "They invited me in for a meeting and basically suggested that they'd make it worth my while if I came and worked for them, and asked me to name a figure," she said. In the end, she declined.

Some Icelanders believed that their country's bankers and entrepreneurs were getting too rich too fast, embracing global wealth with little discipline or foresight about what they would do if the economy turned sour. But Icelanders have long prided themselves on possessing the grit essential for survival on a remote island devoid of lush forests or fertile prairies. And perhaps because for centuries Icelanders were desperately and chronically poor, the newfound prosperity seemed to signal that the nation had left its troubles behind.

Within a generation, the explosion of new wealth had transformed Iceland into a place infatuated with money. The strength of the krona made imported goods easily affordable. Container ships loaded with luxury consumer goods began arriving at Iceland's ports, disgorging high-end Scandinavian furniture, Range Rovers, flat-screen TVs, building materials for houses, and countless other signs of ebullient spending. On top of the egregious domestic consumption were investments abroad in second and third homes, even high-end condo developments in New York, British soccer teams, and department stores.

Here is what overconnectivity can yield: by 2007, Icelanders owned about fifty times more foreign assets than they had five years earlier.

Paradoxically, however, the key ingredient in keeping the krona so strong—the high interest rates—was posing a problem for small companies and the general public. The high interest rates made loans very expensive. To get around this issue, the banks began to offer "currency basket" loans denominated in currencies of other countries, where interest rates were lower. That is, you could fill your loan basket almost as you wished—say, with 30 percent yen, 30 percent euros, and the rest with Swiss francs—all at far lower interest rates than borrowing kronur would cost.

Many ordinary Icelanders jumped on the debt bandwagon, and suddenly naïve consumers had unwittingly become currency speculators who were about to get their clocks cleaned. They had become connected—overconnected—to international financial markets. In 2006 and 2007, currency basket loans were all the rage. The prevailing sentiment was that taking a currency basket loan was the only sane thing to do in that economic climate. Alda described the situation well: "We could shop for a car or a house online, then with one click of the mouse transfer to our bank's Web site and calculate how high the monthly payments would be with a currency basket loan," she said. "Two hours later we could be at the car dealership, and the salesman could finalize the loan deal almost instantly. Meanwhile, there was no warning anywhere about the risk of taking such a loan. It was crazy."

In the same way that most Icelanders did not understand (or care) how their banks had grown so big, they did not understand the weak basis of their currency, or that it might take a sudden nosedive. This weakness meant that if the krona dropped precipitously but the currency in which the loan had been taken maintained its value, the principal on the loan, or the value of the amount owed, would rise correspondingly. In other words, Icelandic borrowers might need three kronur to pay for every one krona they had borrowed. The Icelandic consumers had become connected to a new environment that they did not understand. Indeed, by mid-2009 the citizens of Iceland owed—collectively—more than $900 million in foreign currency for car loans alone, and 11 percent of households were paying more than 30 percent of their disposable income toward those loans.

The collapse of Lehman Brothers in September 2008 started a tremor that augured a global crisis of confidence, with the once-isolated island of Iceland at the center of it all. To make a large foreign loan payment that was coming due in mid-October, Glitnir had been planning to make an asset sale. But when Lehman failed, the sale fell apart. To make matters worse, the bank found itself unable to renew a bank loan it had counted on being extended. Collapse was now certain, and the government stepped in to take a controlling interest in the failing bank.

One factor in the banking madness, perhaps overlooked by pundits, is that Icelanders are by habit prone to excess. For most Icelanders a conservative banker's personality is a misfit. Having been dependent on fishing for so long, Icelanders are accustomed to "binge working." That is, they worked when the boats came in with the catch, and everyone in the community was called out to help—even the schools were closed—until the valuables had been preserved. Icelanders also party excessively, at least in Alda's view. And they are terrible drivers, paying scant attention to the rules of the road and apt to park their cars anywhere at all. Much of this, says Alda, has to do with their irreverent nature. One of the most popular Icelandic expressions is *thetta reddast*, which means essentially, "it will all work out one way or another." Icelanders tend to invoke that sentiment in just about any situation, no matter how dire, and it is likely that many of the risk-happy bankers dismissed any nagging fears or doubts with just that adage. *Thetta redast* is to the Icelanders what *mañana* is to the Spanish.

But the developing financial crisis was not so easily ignored by others. Creditors—dozens of British and Dutch municipalities, banks, and hedge funds around the world that used Iceland's high interest rates and high-flying currency to power returns—were owed more than $70 billion. And when these foreign investors tried to pull out—converting kronur back into dollars or euros en masse—the currency fell like a rock. As word of the devaluation spread, it spurred more withdrawals, and the unraveling of the nation's economy began in earnest. The run on the bank had become a run on the nation. A positive feedback process just ran wild and swept away a country.

The domino effect was swift. On the afternoon of October 6, 2008, the prime minister, Geir Haarde, addressed the nation on television to announce plans for an emergency bill allowing nationalization of the other failing Icelandic banks.

When investors around the world began to panic in the autumn of 2008, SWIFT was there to carry the telecommunications freight. Throughout September, in the midst of a high degree of market volatility following the collapse of Lehman Brothers, SWIFT experienced some of the most heavily trafficked days in its history. The situation got more interesting in October as the capital markets continued to decline, and in the wake of the Iceland collapse, SWIFT experienced record-breaking message volumes in two back-to-back days—October 14 and 15—with more than seventeen million messages carried on each of those days.

SWIFT officials took credit for keeping the transaction process functioning smoothly. By 2008, SWIFT was working with nearly nine thousand financial institutions and businesses to "carry out their business operations with certainty," as the 2008 annual report stated, with a major portion of SWIFT's business "involved with facilitating financial transactions over the Internet."

SWIFT provided "operational certainty during the height of the crisis and beyond Iceland." That is to say, SWIFT worked to make certain the three bankrupt banks could send and receive SWIFT messages.

At the same time, depositors in Icesave and Kaupthing Edge, most of them in the U.K., were in full panic mode. Amid news that Landsbanki had gone into receivership, the Icesave Web site shut down. Anyone who clicked on it was greeted with this message: "We are not currently processing any deposits or any withdrawal requests through our Icesave Internet accounts. We apologize for any inconvenience this may cause our customers. We hope to provide you with more information shortly." By then it had become evident to many Britons that the Icelandic Deposit Compensation Fund did not have anything close to the necessary reserves to cover the accumulated deposits in Icesave. On Web sites and blogs, people reported feeling physically sick. Many wept uncontrollably as they faced the potential loss of their entire life savings.

With Kaupthing Edge, the situation was slightly more complex, and—as has since come to light—somewhat more sinister. With the collapse of both Glitnir and Landsbanki in Iceland, Kaupthing Edge depositors in Europe were becoming nervous. However, as late as October 7, Kaupthing was still reassuring its customers that the bank was sound. Those who logged on to the Kaupthing main site were greeted with an announcement that a certain Sheik Mohammed Bin Khalifa Al-Thani, brother of the sultan of Qatar, had a few days earlier purchased a 5 percent share in the bank. The announcement was intended to boost consumer confidence in Kaupthing, and it worked. ""When I logged on to the Web site and saw that a member of the Qatar royal family had bought a share in Kaupthing, coupled with a statement of the sheik's confidence in the bank, I was reassured that everything was O.K.," said Jan Flushnik, a German Kaupthing Edge depositor whose savings were trapped inside Edge's virtual vaults from October 2008 until June 2009. An investigation into the bank's activities has since revealed that the Qatar transaction was a sham intended to cover up Kaupthing's precarious position.

Not all Edge depositors were soothed, however. By October 6, 2008, news had spread that Iceland's banks were in trouble. Across Europe, people with their money in Kaupthing Edge scrambled to withdraw their savings. There was a problem, however; the deposits had been electronically transferred to Iceland almost as soon as they had come in, so they were no longer readily available at the Edge outposts to repay the depositors. With the media on their backs and the Financial Supervisory Authority breathing down their necks, Edge managers across Europe frantically attempted to recover the money their clients had entrusted to them.

Then, on October 8, Kaupthing Edge managers were ordered to stop payouts to depositors. The following day, U.K. financial authorities transferred control of Kaupthing Edge to the online bank ING Direct and took further actions that forced the bank's U.K. operation to default on its loans.

On October 9, trading was shut down on the Iceland stock exchange, which had plummeted more than 85 percent. Trading in the krona, which was suddenly essentially worthless outside Iceland, was also stopped.

British officials, in the meantime, were livid. Britons had deposited more than $5 billion in Iceland's online banks. Invoking a relatively new antiterrorism law, the British government declared Iceland a terrorist nation and froze the assets of the two Icelandic banks—Landsbanki and Kaupthing—in the U.K. And by taking control of the British subsidiary of Kaupthing, the last survivor of the three banks, the government automatically triggered the default of its parent company back in Iceland.

The *kreppa*—or "crisis"—was quickly felt by ordinary Icelanders. Those who had taken the currency basket loans were now forced to face the rapidly rising cost of car or home loans. When the economy collapsed and the krona plummeted, they were in big trouble. The loss of value in the krona meant that they needed to use two to four kronur to pay back the foreign currency loans for every krona they had borrowed. Some saw their loans quadruple, and suddenly their car, say, or house, was worth a lot less than the amount of the loan. A home purchased for $500,000 in a foreign currency, for instance, was now sitting under a $1.5 million mortgage because the krona had depreciated. A car bought for $35,000 now had a $100,000 loan. And since Iceland is heavily reliant on imports, the price of many goods shot up. Some foods, like olive oil, for instance, doubled in price almost overnight.

Icelanders living abroad were also in trouble, particularly those who relied on payments from home—primarily students. Immediately after the collapse, as money transfers to and from Iceland virtually stopped, they were left without funds for days and even weeks. Stories emerged about caring neighbors who lent money for food and diapers, or good Samaritans who took up collections to help Icelandic students pay their rent. However, when those problems were resolved, students were forced to come to grips with the fact that the value of their loan contributions—paid in kronur—had plummeted, and they had to struggle to make ends meet as never before.

Ordinary citizens were, understandably, incensed. Most of their banking compatriots, whom they referred to as *útrásarvíkingar*, or modern-day Viking marauders, had fled the country, so the public's fury was directed at the government, the country's regulatory agency (the Financial Supervisory Authority), and the Central Bank of Iceland (the Icelandic equivalent of the Federal Reserve), all of which had failed to protect the nation from calamity. Faced with the collapse of their economy, a massive devaluation of their currency, and a deep fear about what would follow, Icelanders took to the streets in protest. Every Saturday afternoon, demonstrations were held in front of the parliament buildings, where people gathered to find an outlet for their anger and frustration. Initially the prevailing feelings were of a deep and unfocused rage and much confusion. As weeks passed, however, four main demands began to form. With ever-growing anger, the people shouted for the government to resign, for the heads of the Central Bank to resign, for those in charge of the Financial Supervisory Authority to resign, and for new national elections to be held.

Government officials effectively ignored the protests. Stunned into something of a torpor, they tried to work behind closed doors. With Christmas approaching, the number of protesters dwindled, and in December 2008 it appeared that the Icelandic nation would return to its previous indifference. Then, on New Year's Eve, during an annual television program in which the country's political leaders met in a live broadcast from a downtown hotel to discuss the year's events, things came to a head. Demonstrators crowded the hotel and banged on windows, disrupting the broadcast, and someone took wire cutters to one of the broadcast cables. The riot police intervened, using clubs and pepper spray to drive back demonstrators. It was just a small foreshadowing of what was to come.

Three weeks later, as parliament reconvened after the Christmas holidays, furious protesters once again gathered in the square outside the parliament buildings. Part of their rage centered on the program in parliament that day; unemployment was swelling and bankruptcies were on the rise, but on the agenda that day were plans to debate the questions of smoking areas in restaurants and the sale of alcohol in supermarkets. Most people saw these concerns as proof of the total alienation of the country's leadership from its people.

As the parliamentary session began, people started shouting and banging pots and pans outside the parliament building. The cacophony soon morphed into a sort of tribal beat for what would later be dubbed "the kitchenware revolution." By nighttime there were thousands of people outside parliament; someone lit a bonfire; and the chanting of "*Vanhaef ríkisstjórn!!*" ("incompetent government!") became the sonic backdrop to a kind of war dance as people moved and swayed around the fire. Some threw eggs and Skyr—an Icelandic yogurt-like product—at the government buildings and the riot police, who were out in full force. By midnight, the clash reached a new level of violence when a police officer was seriously injured after a protestor hurled a curbstone at him.

Just as cyberspace had helped propel Iceland into a financial crisis, it now fueled the public's outrage. People weren't merely reading news online. They began blogging about what was happening, commenting on news items, posting links to Facebook, and forming protest groups. People started connecting as never before. A movement called Lveldisbyltingin ("the Democratic Revolution") launched a Web site to which people could add their ideas and write about what they thought were the most important issues to address. Out of that Web site, set up in Wiki format, a new political movement began to form. Calling itself the Civic Movement, the Wiki site became a part of its manifesto. The group had no money and was completely grass roots, so its members had to get creative. The group uploaded videos to YouTube and linked to and distributed material on Facebook. And somehow, as often happens in cyberspace, the whole thing just took off; it grew very viral and very contagious very quickly—people distributed material online, blogged energetically about the actions they were taking, and won over the traditional media with their fiery commitment and enthusiasm.

The Civic Movement was not the only campaign born online. The day after the curbstone was thrown, a blog published the identities of police officers and their addresses, urging further violence. Almost immediately, an effort dubbed the Orange Movement was launched on the Internet, exhorting the public to denounce violence against the police. More than a thousand people joined the group on that first day. And in a particularly moving demonstration of the power of the Internet to generate waves, a group of protesters—many of them sporting orange ribbons—broke off from the throng of demonstrators and positioned themselves between the row of riot police and the rest of the crowd, just as violence against the police was heating up again. Three days later, fifteen thousand people—5 percent of the Icelandic nation—had joined the Orange Movement group on Facebook.

The next day, the Icelandic government formally collapsed.

It was a jubilant victory for the thousands of people who by then opposed the government. One of their four demands had now been met; an interim government was installed and elections had been called. Yet back at the Central Bank, Oddsson stubbornly refused to leave his post, despite the pointed call for his resignation by the new prime minister and ongoing loud protests outside the Central Bank. During occasional public appearances Oddsson lashed out at his critics and gave long speeches proclaiming his innocence. In the end, the new prime minister saw no choice but to introduce a bill in parliament giving the government the power to discharge Oddsson. The bill was vehemently opposed by MPs from the Independence Party, who remained fiercely loyal to Oddsson, and it went through lengthy delays before being passed. Oddsson was ousted from the Central Bank in late February, some four weeks after the new government had first requested his resignation.

The overconnection process in Iceland was driven by a dearth of regulation along with dicey policies that have created problems for financiers and bankers for centuries. But all of this would probably have been a nonevent had Iceland's banks remained local. Without the international connections the banks likely would have never amassed assets of much more than $10 billion. When Iceland joined the EEA, it put in place the financial railroad capable of providing access to hundreds of billions of dollars. This action, coupled with recent reforms, created the overconnected state that would ultimately bring Iceland to its knees. The Internet served as the telegraph system that made the railroad much more efficient. Iceland's banks employed strategies that would have been risky at any time in history and that were even less appropriate in the highly connected twenty-first century. Iceland became a victim of the quintessential Internet creation—online banks. The rapid flows of currency were carried on the Internet's communications backbone. Of course, the Internet made possible what may have been history's first electronic run on the banks, when depositors at Icesave and Kaupthing got spooked by rumors. Many of those rumors, and much of the reliable information about the country's problems, traveled to investors on blogs and in electronic newsletters. Everyone and everything was connected via a few mouse clicks.

In late 2009, Icesave delivered the final crushing blow to the citizens of Iceland, when Iceland's parliament succumbed to international pressure and voted to reimburse the British and Dutch governments. At first, the burden fell squarely on the shoulders of Icelandic citizens. But six months later, bowing to pressure from a majority of the Icelandic population, Iceland's president, Ólafur Ragnar Grímsson, vetoed the plan, throwing back into uncertainty just how the country would repay its $6 billion debt to those two countries. The move attracted a great deal of attention and was hailed in some circles as a brave representation of a nation refusing to bail out private enterprises—in this case, its banks.

Of course, Iceland is not alone in what it experienced. The debt crisis that Greece, and by extension the European Union, found itself strapped with early in 2010 is yet another illustration of how the Internet can break you. Many experts blamed Greece's troubles on Greece itself. And, indeed, for years the nation made bad fiscal decisions. Unrestrained spending, irresponsible lending, and failure to implement financial reforms left Greece in precarious straits. By 2009, the nation's debt had grown to nearly $415 billion, larger than the country's economy.

Greece's troubles, however, were made worse by heavy trading in credit default swaps, which effectively allowed speculators to bet on financial disaster. That is, if Greece were to default on its debts, the traders who owned the credit default swaps stood to profit. As one analyst put it, it was like buying fire insurance on your neighbor's house, which you happen to know has a dangerously outdated electrical system, so that you now have a stake in the house burning down. Should the fire occur, you could watch from the safe redoubt of your own intact home, and then collect the insurance.

By early 2010, numerous speculators were betting against an entire national economy. And one of the players facilitating the high-stakes gambling binge was a little-known company called Markit. In late 2009, Markit introduced something called the iTraxx SovX Western Europe index, based on credit default swaps. Composed of more than a dozen swaps, the index made it easier for speculators to bet on Greece going bust. Until iTraxx SovX came along, firms had traded sovereign credit default swaps individually but not in great volume. The Markit index made it easier to aggregate trading by allowing people to buy or sell an entire index, thus making the product much more liquid.

Greece's problems accelerated at an astonishing rate. The iTraxx SovX index was created on September 28, 2009, and within four months it appeared to have some role in Greece's problems. The crisis in Greece was also a powerful example of positive feedback. As banks and others rushed into trading the iTraxx SovX index, the cost of insuring Greece's debt rose. Alarmed by that bearish signal, bond investors then shunned Greek bonds, making it harder for the country to borrow. That development compounded the anxiety, accelerating the entire problem.

Such global trading would have been difficult if not impossible to pull off in an Internet-free world. Like nearly every other financial services company, Markit relied heavily on the Internet and its underlying protocols for sending and receiving data, and for executing transactions. The Internet made it possible to make big, instantaneous bets on the emerging crisis.

Of course, overconnection also played a large role in the subprime meltdown in the U.S. Many middle-class Americans who are now looking for jobs at living wages are being affected by overconnection in ways very similar to the nation of Greece and to Icelanders who took to the streets.

New levels of connectivity put all of us in contact with new environments. Adjusting to those environments is very difficult, whether you are a nation, a government, a social or economic institution, or an individual living in Reykjavík, Moscow, Athens, or Portland, Maine. The ease with which you can end up insolvent is in large part due to the lack of friction in the system. And friction-free systems can catch you completely unawares.

Kristján Davídsson, for his part, did not for one minute see the collapse coming. The day before the government seized control of Glitnir he spoke at an aquaculture conference in Norway, and it was, he recalled, "business as usual." The following week, he was being told to look for another job. When Alda spoke with him a year later, Kristján said he could never imagine going back to his tiny home town. Perhaps he feels so because of the intensity of his stint at Glitnir and the shrinking of the world through all his connections. Kristján is, like so many of us, a product of the twenty-first century's cult of connectivity and a paradigm of how we cannot return to the past. "Being a fisherman is, in many ways, a worry-free life—you leave your concerns behind on the pier when you go out to sea because out there there's nothing you can do about anything, anyway. But once you leave the place, like I did—that life is no longer an option. You can't go back. Are you going to offer your spouse, who probably has her own education, that as an option? Do you want your kids to grow up there? No, I could not go back."

NINE

Positive Feedback and Horrendous Financial Crashes

Financial booms, busts, swindles, and contagions have been with us for centuries. As interconnectivity has increased, those phenomena have grown in size and are more likely to span the globe, devastating distant economies. Once I began to understand the implications of overconnectivity, one of the first places I examined for evidence to support my ideas was financial markets. The number of connections in these markets had obviously been growing rapidly in recent years. And once I thought about it a little more, I realized that the danger had also been mounting for years.

I joined Intel, a semiconductor manufacturer, in 1973. Two years earlier, Intel had introduced the microprocessor, a single piece of silicon etched with thousands of tiny transistors and containing all the central works of a computer. I went to work at Intel to run the microprocessor division, and in the eleven years I spent there I was part of a fraternity that prided itself on vision. But that vision focused more on the technology itself than on its social and economic effects. It was easy enough to anticipate dozens of ways a microprocessor could be used: traffic lights would be better able to sense their environment and improve the flow of traffic; cash registers would become smarter, capable of adding sales tax directly to the bill; and airplanes would have improved control systems. We talked a lot about home computers. Some of us envisioned using them to write checks. Perhaps not surprisingly, one of the frequently talked about applications concerned wives keeping recipes on them in the kitchen; how 1970 that was and how sexist, especially considering it's perhaps the one application we foresaw that has never developed in any significant way. We predicted that the performance of these tiny devices would increase exponentially, because, like everyone in the computer industry, and especially those of us in the semiconductor sector (semiconductors being the class of solids out of which transistors are made), we were familiar with what is now known as Moore's law. In 1965, Gordon Moore, an Intel cofounder, made his observation that the number of transistors that can be placed on a computer chip doubles roughly every two years.

That much we knew. But none of us at Intel—from the lowest-ranking salespeople to the highest-level executives—possessed the imagination to predict that Moore's law would continue for the next four decades, with storage capacity increasing by multiple millions. Nor, of course, did we understand the extraordinary impact of such increases in power and decreases in cost. To put it in perspective, the machine that is widely considered to be the first personal computer, called the Altair, had 256 bytes of memory, meaning that it was full to bursting if it tried to hold so much as Matsuo Basho's famous frog haiku:

> *an ancient pond,*
> *a frog jumps in*
> *the splash of water.*

By 2008, the main memory capacity of a microprocessor was a gigabyte, enough to store all eight thousand volumes contained in the Middletown, Ohio, public library. Add some inexpensive disc storage to that, and one system can hold all the words in all the books in five hundred Middletown libraries.

At their best, engineers are inveterate optimists. We Intel

engineers believed our tiny device would improve the world, but we failed to understand how it would transform it. We mused about personal computers (quaintly enough, we called them "microcomputers"). But none of us would have predicted that families would one day sprinkle their homes with such machines.

Nor did we predict the far-reaching effects of the Internet, which originated as such in the early 1970s. True, it was the microprocessor in large part that helped the Internet become so ubiquitous. But if I had made a presentation to the Intel executive staff in the late 1970s suggesting that the microprocessor would some day allow people to listen to thousands of songs on devices that fit into their palms, watch movies on phones that they carried around in their pockets, use those same phones to send little smiley faces from San Jose to Taipei, and find a Saturday night date, someone probably would have left the room, ever so discreetly, to start an immediate search for my replacement. Then again, in 1910, the same skeptical eye would have been cast on overly zealous boosters of the automobile, which gave us the freedom to go where we wanted when we wanted, which created the suburbs, and which served as the backbone of much of the prosperity boom of the twentieth century. Nor would anyone have foreseen its grim side effects—urban sprawl, long commutes, dependence on unstable political regimes for fossil fuels, pollution, and hollowed-out cities. And now we have the Internet, whose side effects we are experiencing like nothing else in the past.

At Intel, we spent a lot of time talking to financial companies about how to use microprocessors to facilitate the trading of currency and stocks over data networks. During one memorable dinner with executives from Reuters, I learned how that company, early in its history, had used carrier pigeons to get the news first. It was obvious that if carrier pigeons created a competitive advantage for Reuters and its customers, microprocessors and data networks would be much more powerful.

In the ensuing years, out of sheer curiosity I read some remarkable theoretical studies of financial contagions and plowed through some hairsplitting texts by economists disagreeing over whether X was correlated enough to Y to qualify as a contagion. As an outsider (i.e., not an economist) who happened to be witnessing firsthand the increasing number of interconnections being brought about by microprocessors, I kept thinking to myself that tight coupling increased the chances for creating massive amounts of positive feedback in a system, which in turn would drive things to extremes, making financial markets less predictable.

When large amounts of positive feedback are present, change proceeds very rapidly—sometimes before anyone has a chance to understand what is happening—with results that are especially unpredictable. For economists and policy makers this rapid change can be especially vexing. The experts' convictions might be firm, but they can't predict the results of even the most carefully planned action.

As we now know, positive feedback drives things to extremes, and when those extremes are reached, we can become very vulnerable. Positive feedback helps create businesses that are too big to fail and too complex to manage. One can therefore expect to see the development of oligopolies and monopolies—and extreme business conditions. Customers become vulnerable to the whims of powerful corporations.

What I discovered about financial manias, panics, bubbles, and crashes was that, while each is unique, they all share common elements, like a dependence on interconnectivity. At some phase of each, positive feedback fuels greed and drives prices to unrealistic highs. It gives rise to feverish investing. It also amplifies fear during a decline and drives prices to unimaginable lows. The same feverish investors then dispose of assets at dirt-cheap prices. Sometimes a precipitous decline, such as the 1987 stock market crash, is triggered by an accident. More often, declines occur when investors demand a return of their money. Bernie Madoff's massive Ponzi scheme fell apart when his customers demanded the return of billions of dollars.

In 1720 John Law's Mississippi scheme began to unravel when Law refused an investment from the Prince de Conti and, to spite Law, de Conti sent three wagonloads of notes to his bank and demanded payment in coin.

When we look back on such disasters, we are always amazed at the miscalculations, irrational behavior, bad judgment, and naïveté of investors. Sometimes the contagion takes on almost comic proportions, as it did in the Dutch tulip mania, when a simple sailor brought to a wealthy merchant news of the arrival of valuable cargo and was rewarded with a fine red herring. Seeing a tulip bulb on the counter among silks and velvets, he mistook it for an onion and slipped it into his pocket to use as an embellishment of the herring's flavor. A short while later, that same merchant, now furious, searched the waterfront for the thief. He found the sailor sitting innocently on a coil of ropes eating a Semper Augustus tulip bulb, worth three thousand florins. Such an incident prompts one to wonder why the merchant did not see what a ridiculous extreme the mania had reached and sell off his tulip holdings. The "tulip onion" should have served as a harbinger of the collapse.

What distinguishes most modern-day crises from their pre–Information Age predecessors is the sheer number of people and economies they affect. The seventeenth-century Dutch tulip mania swept through Holland but didn't travel much farther. Jobbers in London and Paris attempted to spread the craze but were only modestly successful. Those within Holland, however, were caught up in the mania; even the poor joined the craze. As the thought contagion spread, people decorated their clothing and homes with tulip designs. Others speculated their way into deep debt. In the fall of 1636, at the height of the craze, a single bulb could bring thousands of dollars. Then, just months later, in February 1637, the tulip market imploded when traders were no longer able to find buyers willing to pay the inflated prices; within a few days prices dropped 90 percent.

Then there was the South Sea bubble of 1720, which bears an

eerie resemblance to the Internet bubble that followed almost three hundred years later. The South Sea scheme was initially presented to the English parliament by Sir John Blount, a London stockbroker and former scrivener. It called for the newly formed South Sea Company, organized by a large group of London merchants, to buy £9 million of England's national debt, with the government agreeing to pay the company 6 percent interest. As part of the arrangement, the British also gave the company exclusive trading rights to four ports in Spain, with the suggestion that the Crown would subsequently award additional trading rights to a number of South American countries, where, it was rumored, there were vast deposits of gold and other treasures. With an income of more than £500,000 in interest guaranteed annually, and access to the riches of the New World, the South Sea Company began selling its shares on the open market. Investors, convinced of the company's huge potential, drove the stock price up tenfold in a few months.

Meanwhile, to take advantage of the investment frenzy, a number of other businesses were formed. One promised to extract silver from lead, another to strain gold from seawater. Only a few of these enterprises eventually succeeded, and most disappeared as quickly as they had materialized. Still, over the years the South Sea Company managed to sustain excitement in its offerings, making many of its founders fabulously rich. By 1720, however, interest had soured, investors were selling stock at pennies on the pound, and thousands were left in financial ruin.

In 2000 the Internet bubble burst. What happened during the inflation of the prices of Internet stocks looks as irrational as what went on during the South Sea bubble. Some entrepreneurs made fortunes taking public Internet companies that later went bankrupt when revenues failed to develop. Boo.com, an online fashion store, is a famous example. Others came with schemes nearly as farfetched as "straining gold from seawater." The standard promise from entrepreneurs was that they would capture eyeballs—viewers on the Internet—and then figure out how to make money having done so. Maybe they could sell advertising, storage capacity, or some means for searching. My own venture capital firm evaluated but never invested in Napster, a music-sharing site that thought it could make money by permitting college students to make illegal copies of songs using the Internet. The recording companies fought back, and Napster was eventually unable to strain the gold from the unsanctioned transfer of music. In 2001, using overvalued stock, America Online merged with Time Warner, a company with a sustainable business model, in a transaction valued at $350 billion. The combined companies had revenues of around $30 billion, and AOL shareholders owned the majority of the new company. Within a few years AOL's business was in precipitous decline, its dial-up Web access service a victim of much faster broadband technologies. Management was soon searching for ways to spin off AOL.

The dotcom bust was the first large financial crisis in which the Internet played a key role. In fact, the Internet is what we have to thank for spreading much of the thought contagion that created the bubble in the first place and illustrating how thought contagions can take hold and spread in a hyper-interconnected world. Among the earliest infected by this contagion were Internet enthusiasts themselves, who spent hours online participating in chat rooms, gathering information about stocks, learning about technology companies, posting on message boards, reporting facts, spreading rumors, and, in some cases where they had a vested interest, telling blatant lies; they were trading stocks from home and at their desks at work. This widespread—and very speedy—communication among those savvy about the Internet played an important role in the initial boost of technology stocks and subsequently in driving the price of these equities higher and higher. John Doerr, the high-tech venture capitalist, presciently called the Internet "the greatest wealth-creating machine in the history of the world."

Word of huge gains, of 20, 50, 100, and 200 percent, infected the minds of many other individual investors, prompting some to throw out everything they had learned about maintaining a diverse portfolio and invest primarily in high-tech stocks. The demand from these investors put conservative brokers and financial managers in an awkward position: They could either "go with the flow" and put their clients' portfolios at risk by investing heavily in tech stocks, or they could counsel against doing so and risk losing their clients to other, more technology-enlightened advisers. In the end, many brokers and small investors alike were infected by the contagion.

The Internet was also the engine that powered the online trading of stocks. It gave birth to day traders, many of whom quit their jobs to trade from their home or, if they still worked, from their desks at the office. Some of them made hundreds of trades in a single day.

Day trading would never have made sense for small traders before the Internet. The cost of transactions was just too high. In the past you had to give your order to buy or sell a stock to a broker. The commission for each transaction was frequently hundreds of dollars. Thus to make a hundred trades in a day might have cost thousands of dollars and eat up all of a day traders profits.

But the Internet gave rise to online trading services such as E*Trade, Schwab, and Ameritrade, whose discounted services lowered the cost of buying and selling stocks to as little as $5 per transaction. Frantic trading among day traders helped drive tech-stock prices higher. And Wall Street analysts, who should have been a sobering influence, joined in the hysteria.

At the same time, large institutional investors, while hardly immune to the contagion, began to raise red flags. The price of technology stocks was simply climbing too fast, they warned, and corporate valuations that resulted were inflated to points that seemed comical. So strong was the contagion, however, that even when institutional investors pulled out of some stocks completely, enough true believers still remained among smaller investors to drive prices even higher. When the bubble finally burst, the same contagion that served to drive prices up drove them back down. A positive feedback process accelerated the death spiral, and NASDAQ stocks declined by 80 percent over the next three years. After stock market prices came tumbling down, many people had lost their fortunes and their retirement nest eggs.

I too took a hit in the dotcom bust. In 1990, I was the initial investor in a semiconductor start-up called Rambus (whose purpose was to improve the performance of memory chips) and served as chairman of the board for fifteen years. In 1997, the company went public and soon became the darling of both institutional shareholders and dedicated individual investors. Over the next few years I watched the stock climb to $25 and then, at the height of the bubble, top $110, only to fall within the year to less than $4. Meanwhile, as the chairman, I sat by and watched. I wanted management to hold its stock, and I felt committed to setting an example by not selling my own.

Many Rambus investors followed the stock on a Yahoo! message board and over the years posted more than a million messages, filled with truths, rumors, and wishful thinking. Rambus's competitors used the message boards to post savage attacks on the company. Today, the message board still lives on a site called Investor Village, where it is the top forum on the site and where more than four hundred thousand messages have been posted. The stock is now trading at around $20, and the Investor Village message board occasionally carries rumors of a ride to $40, $100, and, fancifully enough, perhaps even $1,000. I still own Rambus stock and am devoted to the company, but I realize now how capricious some of my dreams were.

Of course, the source of the dot-com bubble was our fascination with the Internet and its power. Consumers had fallen in love with Amazon, Yahoo!, and eBay, and people were beginning to get their news over the Internet. Anyone with the slightest imagination could see its potential. If our infatuation had been the only force, the bubble would have been like many other Wall Street bubbles. What was unique about the Internet bubble was that the Internet served as both the object and the medium of our passion. We fell in love with Internet start-ups, and the Internet itself was our aphrodisiac.

By sending us messages that wore away our resistance, the Internet heightened our infatuation beyond all reason.

One of the keys to moderating contagions, in order to prevent runs on banks and the downward spiral in prices when a bubble bursts, is to cure the thought contagion that exacerbates fear. In 1893, Isaias Hellman stopped a potential run on the Farmers and Merchants Bank in Los Angeles by withdrawing $500,000 in gold from his own account at the Nevada Bank in San Francisco, transporting the coins on an overnight train to Los Angeles, and piling them on the bank's counter so customers could see that their withdrawal demands could be met. With that action he quelled the panic.

Of course, slowing a stampede isn't easy. Lemmings really do dive off cliffs. And often enough, stopping a herd isn't in the interest of those in a position to do so. Certainly the royalty in France had no interest in slowing down John Law's Mississippi scheme. As a matter of fact, the royalty was eager to profit from the game.

This fabled intrigue is one of the most colorful and notorious examples of a thought contagion and positive feedback run amok. It was perpetrated on the French upper classes in the early eighteenth century. It ultimately led to financial disaster for many wealthy patricians and sparked an inflation that punished the poor. The scheme was created by a convicted British murderer and prison escapee named John Law. A banker's son and a renowned ladies' man, Law shot a man to death in a duel over the charms of a certain Elizabeth Villiers, later, as Elizabeth Hamilton, Countess of Orkney, a lady-in-waiting to Queen Mary II. Fleeing to the continent, Law took shelter in the French court, where he managed to persuade some new and influential friends that paper money supported by metallic currency, or specie, could become a vehicle for restoring France's credit, then at a low ebb among European nations. In 1716, the court issued a royal edict allowing Law and his brother to establish a bank, subsequently called the Banque Royale, which soon was issuing paper notes well in excess of the value of the specie in the bank's possession.

The following year, Law leveraged his position in the bank to acquire a controlling interest in the derelict Mississippi Company, which had a monopoly on trade with French Louisiana, a region reputed to abound in precious metals and beaver.

In 1719, Law's company, ultimately reorganized as the Compagnie des Indes, began floating stock accompanied by a paper currency issue. Driven by speculators responding to Law's advertising—which touted Louisiana as a treasure trove of rare gems and metals—the price of the company's stock quickly rose from five hundred to ten thousand livres—the eighteenth-century currency of France. Owing in large part to the number of notes issued and the heavy trading activity in the stock, the amount of money circulating through the French economy almost tripled in a year's time, with prices in Paris doubling between May 1719 and December 1720.

Driven by positive feedback, Law's scheme provided him with what seemed like an endless supply of money. The more money his bank printed, the more currency was available for buying shares in his company. The greater the demand for the shares, the higher their price, and the more specie the bank would receive in exchange for its notes. This clever positive feedback system would itself have been enough to drive up the price of the Compagnie shares, just as it drove up prices in Paris. But there was another loop at work as well—the self-fulfilling prophecy, again abetted by Law's advertising campaign as well as increasing word of mouth, that the Compagnie was a smart, moneymaking investment. As the price of the stock rose, people fell over themselves to buy it, further driving up the price and generating even more demand for the shares that had been issued.

Bubbles and manias depend on thought contagions, and Law certainly knew how to create one. Dukes, marquises, and counts waited in the streets outside Law's residence to find out whether he had put their name on the list for stock as it became available, with some even renting nearby apartments so they could be closer to the man himself. One woman went so far as to have her coachman stage a carriage accident when she spotted Law so that he would have occasion to speak with her. So impressed was Law when she confessed her ploy that he put her on the list.

Even the most productive money machines will stop when people become suspicious. Law discovered this when he refused to sell shares to the Prince de Conti at a price the prince deemed fair. This rebuff was an "accident" that brought Law's perpetual motion machine to a screeching halt. Irate, the prince sent three wagons of notes and demanded payment in specie. Learning of the prince's actions, others began to ask for specie payment for their notes. This development caused the stock price to fall at the same time it made finding buyers increasingly difficult.

The inability to meet the demand for specie created a panic. Soon payment in specie was stopped altogether.

To buoy flagging investor confidence, Law recruited more than 5,000 down-and-out Parisians to work in the Louisiana gold fields, then marched his pick-and-shovel crew through the city's streets. Two-thirds of these conscripts immediately vanished into the French countryside, where more than a few sold their tools for whatever they could get. Many were back in Paris within a month, having never set foot in one of Louisiana's fabled mines.

It was, in any event, too late for Law's mock parade to restore confidence, and before long the crowds at the bank's door, still demanding specie, grew so violent that a dozen people were crushed to death. Not long after, the company collapsed.

Although the Mississippi scheme, the tulip mania, and the South Sea bubble occurred centuries ago, the positive feedback processes that fueled their growth and drove their demise are still powerful forces to be reckoned with in the overconnected world. Today those processes no longer depend on discussions at sidewalk cafés in Paris, physical meetings in offices on Lombard Street, or banknotes carried in wheelbarrows. As we shall shortly see, the 2008 financial meltdown was driven by a much more complex set of feedback mechanisms, most of them powered by the Internet.

TEN

How the Internet Supercharged the Subprime Crisis

To see the recent subprime crisis coming should not have taken a genius. Ignoring its prospect was like looking at a forest blanketed with dead underbrush and dying trees—in drought season—and not being concerned about a forest fire. Of course, no one can predict when such a fire will occur. But the chances that one will happen are extremely high.

The underbrush prior to the subprime crisis was the large number of important positive feedback loops—tens, probably hundreds of them—driving the financial system to extremes and creating thought contagions that inspired greed. They were making the system more volatile and less predictable and creating an accident-prone environment as vulnerable as a dry forest floor. It was certain that someone would drop a lit match eventually; the only question was when. However, people found it hard to pack up and leave, because if you sold your investments too early in the cycle you stood to miss out on making very big money.

Did I see the danger of continuing to camp in the forest? I was no genius. I created a very diversified portfolio and was pretty conservative in my asset allocation. But I failed to see how dry the underbrush was—that is, the degree of interconnection among all the loops. I did well enough to feel smarter than most of the crowd, but, in the end, I lost enough to get quite badly burned.

What were the positive feedback loops that formed the under-brush? Whenever I think about them, the words of a banker I spoke with shortly after the 2008 crash echo in my mind: "It could not have happened without the Internet." She meant that the Internet made things worse. As I keep pointing out, increasing the amount of positive feedback in a system just a little bit makes things happen much faster, for better or worse. The compounding of money is a positive feed-back process everyone has experienced in one way or another. If the yield on an investment goes from 5 percent to 8 percent, your money doubles in nine years instead of fourteen. Adding just a little more gain—for instance, increasing the interest rate by 3 percent—makes things get much bigger much more quickly. My banker friend was saying that the Internet supercharged the positive feedback processes that were already in place, making them far more combustible.

Two particularly volatile, interconnected positive feedback loops were the Subprime Credit Positive Feedback Loop and the Asian Offshore Manufacturing Positive Feedback Loop. I focus on this con-nection particularly because it is so obvious, yet few have commented on it. It is also one that was powered in a significant way by the Internet. Of course, the Subprime Loop interacted with a lot of other positive feedback loops as well, such as the one in which mortgages were bundled together and sold as securities by investment banks like Goldman Sachs. In turn, one of the reasons Goldman and others were able to pull off these transactions is that they were part of what one might name the Shadow Bank Positive Feedback Loop. All such loops were powered by what we'll call the Financial System Egregious Compensation Positive Feedback Loop. Well, you get the idea.

But let's go back to how the Internet facilitated growth in the sub-prime mortgage market. Customers could shop online for the best mort-gage deals. This activity made the market more competitive and drove mortgage brokers to respond more quickly, without proper evaluation of the deals. Not long ago, I met a former property appraiser who had gotten out of the business because it had become so irrational. He was now driving a limo, finding his appraisal methods outdated. Mortgage brokers and banks had taken to shopping for appraisers on the Internet, and an appraiser would get hired based on his initial guess at what the property was worth. Brokers preferred appraisers who were likely to give them the highest appraisal. In this way the Internet helped raise the value of appraisals—adding gain to the system.

The appraiser now driving a limo could no longer compete. Once the new appraisers got the job, they could carry out the work in a few hours—not by getting in their cars and looking at the properties in question, then examining comparable sales in the neighborhood. All they had to do was fire up MapQuest and compare equivalent sale prices nearby, all without leaving their offices. And if the Internet real estate listing said a property had a view, they duly noted that feature without question. Again, the Internet had added fuel to the fire—raising values by streamlining the appraising process.

Once the property was appraised, more automated systems took over. In the 1990s, Bill Kelvie, the chief information officer of Fannie Mae and an acquaintance of mine, directed the development of Internet-based tools that made possible instant loan approval. This system was tied to a suite of supporting software systems for the process of pricing and delivery of loans, automated underwriting, loss mitigation, and credit modeling. These no doubt did a better job than most administrative employees would have, but by speeding up the process they heightened the fever possessing the real estate market. They thereby abetted the thought contagion that sustained the housing bubble, adding more positive feedback to the system.

Once the basic homework was done, all that remained for the mortgage to be granted was the mundane paperwork. The Internet helped that, too. Electronic documents would fly through the system, compressing into hours paperwork that had once taken days. Too many buyers, inflamed by the vision of owning their first houses, did not have time to reflect. Like the Icelanders signing up for the "currency basket" loans, they thoughtlessly signed on the bottom line.

Cheap money also made the process work so well. Countrywide, Washington Mutual, and other lenders could originate mortgages and sell them to people who could afford them only if borrowing rates were low at first. Such cheap money was a result of decisions made by the Federal Reserve to keep interest rates low, as well as what I call the Asian Savings Glut. Here's how that worked: unlike Americans, workers in Asia are great savers. Some of them save 30 percent or more of what they earn. That money was looking for safe places that paid reasonable interest. A lot of money flowed back to the U.S. when China bought Treasury, Fannie Mae, and Freddie Mac bonds, as well as stakes in hedge funds and in investment banks like Morgan Stanley. So, in essence, wages paid to factory workers in Asia kept interest rates in the U.S. low and helped fund subprime loans.

What kicked in next was the Security Securitization Positive Feedback Loop: mortgage originators who charged high fees were motivated to sell mortgages to even the least creditworthy customers. They then sold the mortgages to banks and investment banks that created collateralized debt obligations (CDOs). These CDOs are bundles of mortgages merged into a single package and then sold to investors. For example, you might take one thousand mortgages of, say, $250,000 each (the collateralized debt) and create a $250 million CDO that you then sell to investors. So the home owners make payments to the mortgage originators, which pass the money on to the investment banks, which in turn make payments to the holders of the CDOs.

If this process seems complicated, just think how cumbersome it would have been without the Internet. Electronic payments made the process simpler, faster, and easier to navigate. Bankers could wire money within minutes. Payments could be made from borrowers' bank accounts automatically, and banks could wire that money to the holders of CDOs. Investment banks made big fees selling those CDOs to investors such as hedge funds and pension plans. These buyers loved the CDOs, because they were engineered to pay high interest and to appear secure. To make them so, all it took was a little creative financial engineering.

This "engineering" began with the investment banks creating so-called tranches (from French, meaning "slices") of debt. The safest mortgages were put in one tranche, the less safe ones in another, and the least safe in still another. The safest tranche paid the least interest, while the riskiest paid the highest.

Now the trick was to find a way to make the riskiest debt, the subprime pools of mortgages, as safe an investment as high-quality corporate debt—nothing but a little alchemy to turn mortgage lead into mortgage gold. This is where companies like American International Group, Inc., came in.

AIG was an insurance company with a sterling credit rating of triple A—the best. If AIG were to insure the low-quality debt, the company's sterling credit rating would adhere to the debt. This indeed is what happened in many cases. As a result, some very risky CDOs, insured by AIG, were designated triple A by credit-rating services such as Standard & Poor's and Moody's.

So what I call the Security Securitization Positive Feedback Loop worked by creating CDOs that paid high interest and appeared to be safe. And indeed they were safe as long as AIG did not fail. These safe-appearing CDOs were then sold by the investment banks to hedge funds, retirement funds, and other sophisticated investors. To make the CDOs even more appealing, the investment banks that sold them lent money at attractive rates to the hedge funds so they could buy them. In no time, a thought contagion broke out. Since everyone was doing it and since few truly safe investments were paying as high an interest rate at the time, buying "safe" CDOs with borrowed money became the smart thing to do. This reasoning is just another example of a positive feedback loop reinforcing another positive feedback loop.

The Internet, of course, also helped to create the CDOs and market them. That is, the high demand for high-interest-paying, safe

CDOs raised the demand for subprime mortgages, which led to even more reckless practices on the part of mortgage originators. And so things escalated. More and more consumers were lining up for such loans. Was their credit shaky and did they lack steady income? No problem! So-called no doc loans (requiring no documentation of income) became increasingly routine. What could be better than paying no money down and getting a low starter rate without even having to prove your income? With such deals available, it was often cheaper to buy a house than to rent, at least initially.

What also made all of this work so well was cheap money available because of the Asian savings glut. The Asian Off-Shore Manufacturing Positive Feedback Loop glut was critical to creating the savings glut.

We have the Internet to thank for ramping up this phenomenon. It did this in a number of ways. For one thing, it eased the sharing of information with subcontractors and company-owned facilities in foreign countries. Orders and specifications could be communicated instantly. Production and shipment status could be tracked online. When all was said and done, not only was using offshore labor cheaper, but also coordinating the remote production of TVs, auto parts, and toys was easier. Another advantage is that companies using offshore labor didn't have to worry much about unions, worker safety, or strict environmental laws.

My main point, however, is that wages paid to factory workers in Asia helped fund the risky subprime loans.

Of course, the key to keeping the loop active was using cheap money to create still more money. As we all learn in college economics, when banks lend money, they create money. The Federal Reserve limits the amount that regulated banks can create by establishing capital and reserve requirements. But lots of other ways exist to create money outside of the regulated banking system. This is where what I'll call the Shadow Bank Positive Feedback Loop came into play. Investment banks, being ineffectively controlled, began to act like regulated banks by accumulating money, lending it out, and, in the process, creating money. Since they were free of many of the constraints imposed on more stringently regulated financial institutions, they became known as shadow banks. They took advantage of this lack of regulation and lent about three times as much money for every dollar of capital they held as regulated banks did, so that instead of being leveraged ten to one they were leveraged thirty to one.

The beauty of this system is that some of the money created by the shadow banks was lent to hedge funds, which purchased the CDOs and thus kept the bubble inflating. Here is just another example of one positive feedback loop reinforcing another.

Supporting all of these positive feedback loops was the Financial System Egregious Compensation Loop. This loop was driven by the desire of corporations to pay their executives in the seventy-fifth percentile of executive pay. The banks believed they had to pay their talented executives at this level both to retain and to motivate them. As a result, young hotshot bankers were earning $1 million, $2 million, even $5 million a year.

Paying employees at the seventy-fifth percentile becomes a positive feedback process because when one entity does it, others follow. Pretty soon seventy-fifth-percentile pay becomes the industry average, or the fiftieth percentile, so that companies paying at the seventy-fifth percentile have to raise the absolute amount they pay to remain there. To put it more concretely, if I'm paying my top producers $1 million a year to put them in the seventy-fifth percentile, and banks that want to hold on to their talent have to match me and pay salaries of $1 million, too, then the $1 million that all the top producers are earning becomes average, and in order to pay my people in the seventy-fifth percentile, I have to raise them to $1.2 million a year.

Many of these highly paid young people were prodigious consumers. They purchased expensive homes in the Hamptons, on Long Island, New York, spent thousands on wine at lavish dinners, and built palatial estates in Connecticut. They also tracked the salaries and lavish exploits of their peers in the media. The Internet made a lot of this easy. JobStar offers more than three hundred free online salary surveys. As salaries become more transparent, the competition among high-level executives intensifies, driving the outlandish pay scales ever higher. It's a typical positive feedback loop, but you can't pay higher and higher salaries unless you earn bigger and bigger profits. So management put pressure on these high-priced employees to generate more business, which they could do only by pressuring the mortgage originators to produce more mortgages that could be packaged into CDOs.

At the bottom of this food chain, the subprime originators put pressure on their employees to write more subprime mortgages. These employees responded by coming up with more and more attractive offers to people who could least afford the mortgages. In turn, those who packaged the mortgages into CDOs were pressed to create increasingly risky financial products.

If you think all the foregoing positive feedback loops were the only ones at work, think again. The government played a role, too, and the politics was bipartisan, or, as we say in the tech sector, platform agnostic, with both parties contributing to the problem. Fannie Mae (the Federal National Mortgage Association) was created in 1938 in order to make government-backed mortgages available to low-income families. By 1968 it had grown so large that President Lyndon Johnson converted it to a private shareholder-owned, publicly traded company whose debt was still implicitly guaranteed by the government. This implicit government guarantee made Fannie Mae part of a positive feedback process, because the safer the debt appeared, the more people wanted to buy Fannie Mae's debt at extremely advantageous rates. The same was true for Freddie Mac (the Federal Home Loan Mortgage Corporation). By 2002, the Bush administration had become actively involved in "encouraging folks to own their own homes," taking a lot of pride in the fact that home ownership had reached a historic high. However, as John Snow, Bush's treasury secretary, later pointed out,

"We forgot in the process" that people have to be able to afford their houses. "We now realize there was a high cost."

But you can't blame just Republicans for the consequences. Democrats applied pressure, too. For instance, in 2003, Barney Frank, the ranking member of the House Committee on Financial Services, led a group of Democrats in criticizing the Bush administration's "ineffectiveness" in "getting the voucher system working that would help low-income Americans purchase homes."

So Fannie Mae, Freddie Mac, politicians from both parties, and the government itself all played roles in lending money to consumers who weren't creditworthy, thereby creating still more powerful positive feedback loops

Of course, the Credit Card Positive Feedback Loop was involved in the crisis as well. Here, the Internet was a big facilitator. It helped identify consumers the credit card companies should market to, and it also helped consumers search for the best deals. Credit cards were a perfect match for new home owners. After all, if you were moving from a small apartment to a big new home, you needed furnishings. Using credit cards to finance the purchases was a great way to solve the problem.

If the equity in their home is rising, consumers feel they are getting wealthier and are willing to take on more credit card debt to buy other things, such as home furnishings. The least creditworthy are great customers; they provide a great deal of the credit card companies' profits because they pay the highest interest rates and rack up the highest penalty fees. They frequently miss payments and get hit with big late fees. When the payments are late, the banks raise their interest rates. And those customers are trapped, because if they are behind on payments, it's too risky for another credit card company to take them on, leaving them stuck with their current bank, which is only too happy to gouge them.

The problem with this approach—aside from its questionable ethics—was that consumers who were already struggling when the interest on their variable-rate mortgages rose were further stressed by the demands to make higher credit card payments. The further behind they got in their credit card payments, the higher the interest rates went and the larger the penalty charges became. The interaction of the housing bubble and aggressive credit card marketing had created yet another positive feedback loop.

Some of these positive feedback loops were much more important than others. For example, the subprime crisis caused investors to lose confidence in the stock market. Many panicked and rushed to sell. The Dow Jones average plunged from 13,338 in January 2008 to 6,547 in March 2009—a 50 percent decline, creating more financial distress, forcing people to sell their homes, and further driving down their prices.

There was the derivative debacle as well. Bear in mind that because they derive their value based on fluctuations in the prices of the underlying assets, derivatives tend to be extremely volatile. Although many derivatives were related to insuring the CDOs, there were many others as well. Some were just bets related to the housing market. Others dealt with seemingly unrelated areas. I have no doubt that problems in the derivative market that were not directly related to the subprime market overflowed into the subprime market and exacerbated the crisis.

In case I haven't made this abundantly clear already, I'll reiterate: financial systems are incredibly complicated. Lofti Zadeh, a computer scientist at UC Berkeley, put it well when he observed shortly after the 2008 crisis that when interdependence increases without a commensurate increase in coordination, a system is in danger of failing. Even hundreds of years ago, the simplest systems were filled with intricacies that business leaders, regulators, governments, and potentates did not understand. So, when crises developed, those same leaders had terrible difficulty figuring out what to do. Those in charge of the South Sea Company applied pressure on parliament to pass the Bubble Act in an attempt to put an end to the creation of speculative companies that crimped the flow of cash into its own coffers. Almost before the ink was dry on the act, investors in speculative companies understandably got spooked. What had been occasional requests for liquidity turned into a stampede. The first two victims were companies the South Sea Company had targeted for legal action. As a result of the panic, hundreds of speculators went bankrupt. Subsequently, the South Sea Company became a victim of its own scheme. It got caught in the market collapse, and its stock fell by 80 percent.

In the midst of the subprime meltdown, I decided to read John Kenneth Galbraith's history *The Great Crash—1929*. For the first fifty pages, I thought I was reading a fictionalized version of the 2008 subprime meltdown, with only the names changed to protect the innocent. As I read more about the Depression that followed the 1929 stock market crash, I was amazed that it took years before economists became convinced that tight money policies maintained by the Fed after the market crash slowed economic activity and caused the Depression.

What if the Internet had existed in 1929? There is no way to know, of course, but let's compare the two crashes, 1929 and 2008, and look at the role the Internet played in making things different nearly eight decades after the stock market collapse of 1929.

But first, some context. During the Roaring Twenties, the physical economy drove economic prosperity. Railroads, cars, radio, chemical manufacture, urbanization, and the building of infrastructure to support the automobile fueled a huge growth in domestic output. By 1927 Henry Ford had sold fifteen million cars—one for every other American family. Factories churned out manufactured goods that were exported around the world. And the government adopted a laissez-faire attitude toward business.

Then, in 1929, everything went downhill. After peaking in June, steel production declined, freight shipments dropped, and the housing industry continued a multiyear slump. As it turned out, the stock market crash was what economists call a "lagging indicator." The country had been in a recession for several months before the market collapsed in October.

The 2008 crisis was very different. The buoyant economy was created by aggressive financial innovation and lax monetary policy. The Internet facilitated a creative financing boom. Cheap credit powered a frenzied subprime market, which got a boost from the Internet. The real estate bubble created jobs and wealth that enabled consumers to spend and spend until they were mired in debt. When real estate prices declined, it ended the boom, sending millions of consumers into bankruptcy. And when the subprime market collapsed, it took the financial markets, services, and manufacturing economy down with it.

From 1925 to 1929, powered by a booming industrial economy and financial innovations that increased the demand for stocks, the stock market quadrupled. And just as in 2008, in the 1920s greed and unbridled optimism lifted the stock market to unprecedented altitudes.

The most creative financially engineered instruments of the 1920s were the investment trusts. These trusts sold the public risky common stock along with safe preferred stock in the trust and very safe bonds backed by the trust that paid high interest rates. The trusts then invested the money raised from these sales in the stocks of other companies. It did not take long for financial engineers to come up with the idea of setting up these trusts as pyramids. That is, if you stacked the trusts on top of one another, a 100 percent rise in the price of the underlying stock owned by the trust could result in a quadrupling—or more—in the value of the common shares in the trust. At the same time, if those underlying stocks fell by 50 percent, the common stock of the trust would be worthless. Because of the way the trusts were designed, the preferred shareholders and bond-holders would not lose anything. All of the losses were charged to the common shareholders in the trust.

Goldman Sachs, an agile firm that by 1928 had already been in business for nearly fifty years, quickly learned to play the trust pyramiding game. The company first sold stock in the Goldman Sachs Trading Corporation in December 1928. It used insider buying to drive the price from $100 per share to $222.50, while unloading it on a naïve public on the way up. In July 1929, Goldman founded the creatively financed Shenandoah Corporation and twenty-five days later introduced the Blue Ridge Corporation. Shenandoah purchased most of the common stock in the Blue Ridge financial pyramid. By March 1932, Blue Ridge was trading at $.63 and Shenandoah at $.50.

Trusts created by Goldman Sachs and other Wall Street firms were supercharged moneymaking machines powered by the fuel of a rising market. If the Internet had been around, I am sure the creative financiers at Goldman and other investment banks would have made the trusts available to the entire world. If that had been the case, there would have been more money to drive the stock market up. If that had happened, the market would have had farther to fall and the Great Crash would have seriously injured more investors around the world.

In the twenty-first century, advances in technology facilitated new forms of financial innovation, including high-yield bonds backed by collections of subprime mortgages that gave investors high returns with no apparent risk. Trillions of dollars in complicated financial products were sold in world markets on a huge scale. Without the Internet, it would have been nearly impossible to handle the volume of transactions or process the paperwork involved. Many of the shadow banks behind these transactions—e.g., Lehman Brothers and Bear Stearns—were undercapitalized. In the case of Bear Stearns, if the value of its assets fell by just 3 percent it would teeter on the edge of bankruptcy, which is precisely what happened.

One major difference between the Great Crash and the crisis some eight decades later is that in 1929 only about 1.5 million people owned stock out of a population of 120 million, and this stock ownership was concentrated in the hands of the wealthy. As a result, the decline in the stock market had a direct effect on the net worth of only a relatively small percentage of the population. If the Internet had existed in 1929, there is little doubt that a much larger number of people would have owned stocks. This would have meant that the middle class would have been destroyed not only by the loss of jobs and bank failures but by the disastrous decline in the value of stocks, depressing the economy even more.

In contrast, thanks in large part to the Internet, stock ownership today is very broadly distributed. The typical American might own stock directly in a personal account or a 401(k). Or he might own it indirectly, in his retirement plan. A decade ago, seventy million Americans owned stock, and some people estimate that more than half the population is directly vulnerable to market downturns. So the recent decline in both the stock market and the housing market affected the wealth of a large proportion of the population. They no longer had the money to spend to keep the economy humming.

Remember the hot money that rushed in and out of Iceland? Such a thing existed in the 1920s, too. There was a lot of hot money seeking high returns on safe loans. Prior to the Great Crash, the interest rates on "call money"—money lent to investors to purchase stock on margin—frequently exceeded 10 percent. These were very safe loans, because they were backed by stocks that the brokerage firms sold out from under investors when the stock declined. This forced selling drove down the price of stocks. Much of the call money came from corporations and out-of-town banks that concluded they could earn more by lending their capital on Wall Street than by pursuing their traditional businesses or lending to local businesses and consumers. When things started to unwind on October 24, the out-of-town banks and corporations called in $2 billion, creating further pressures on the market.

Before the 2008 crisis, there was lots of hot money floating around. Hedge funds had their money invested in Iceland. Shadow banks had borrowed short term from regulated banks. Hedge funds invested short-term money in exotic financial products. As the crisis unfolded, these same institutions rushed to withdraw their funds. Many of these loans were not rolled over when the crisis hit. This money could vanish in a matter of seconds, transferred over Internet-powered networks.

In 2008, the Internet provided the infrastructure on which new financial products were built and marketed. The Internet helped people buy their homes and shop for loans, and it helped create a frenzy among home buyers. It made the stock market more accessible to investors, so more people tied their financial futures to the price of stocks. As a result, it exposed more people to its decline. It helped to keep interest rates low by playing a role in the Asian savings glut. It helped to keep inflation under control by facilitating world trade and making inexpensive products available in our domestic markets.

Could the subprime crisis and cheap money have happened without the Internet? Sure. But remember, adding just a little bit more positive feedback to a system makes things grow faster and larger. I am convinced that if the Internet had existed in 1929, the market would no doubt have gone higher and fallen farther. More people would have invested in the market and then seen their savings obliterated. There would have been even less money for consumers to spend, and unemployment would have risen beyond the record numbers it hit. So you might just say that in 1929 the country was lucky.

ELEVEN

Positive Feedback and Information Efficiency at Work

In 1956, my junior year at Dartmouth, I took a course from Professor John Adams called "The World Since 1912." Adams gave spellbinding lectures. Students often asked him to hold them on big weekends so they could bring their dates. (Dartmouth was still an all-male school at the time.) There was only one problem with Adams's course. He gave tests that required detailed knowledge of years, names, and places. They were a nightmare of nits. One day a student stood up in the back of class and said: "Professor Adams, I am an engineer. I took this course to broaden myself. It is a great course, but why do I have to memorize all of these facts?" Adams answered without missing a beat: "I have found that the more facts people know, the less they theorize." End of discussion.

Well, I guess I don't know enough facts about the Internet to keep from theorizing, which Professor Adams might well have disapproved of. Still, I can't imagine how many facts it would take to keep me from theorizing that much of what applies to the Internet with regard to finance is also true of aspects of society that have little to do with finance. And that particular theory is backed up by a lot of facts.

What amazes me most about the Internet is the swift and sweeping ways it has affected so many people's lives. We entertain ourselves differently because of the Internet. We shop differently. We get our news differently. We socialize differently. We conduct political campaigns differently. We structure businesses differently. We work differently, and we play differently. We get advice differently, and we give advice differently. The railroad, automobile, telephone, radio, and television all affected us but not as deeply and broadly—and not nearly as quickly.

The connections created by the Internet served to strengthen pre-existing ones. When it did so to large, complex systems, it frequently created positive feedback where none existed before. At other times it increased the amount of positive feedback already present in the system. With this came rapid change. When Amazon.com first went online in 1995, it instantly created a bookstore in every place in the world with an Internet connection. Think of the many decades it took Borders to build the physical infrastructure for its stores. Had the Internet existed before bookstores did, would there have been any reasons to build them? Yes, but not as many. Or think about eBay, which at any given moment is holding millions of auctions—currently more than a hundred million items are listed—everywhere and nowhere.

The Internet not only improves parts of a process, but also in many cases transforms the complete system. Most technologies change and improve bits and pieces of a system but leave the system as a whole pretty much the way it was. For example, when the PC first appeared, two of its first important applications were word processing and spreadsheets. Among other functions, word processing made it easier and more efficient to write newspaper stories, but it did not transform newspapers. I still remember calling on customers when I was with Intel and hearing stories of how reporters wrote their stories on portable PCs and then searched for phone booths so they could file their copy using acoustic couplers—slow, unreliable, and cumbersome devices that transmitted data by feeding tones into the phone. There were still lots of reporters. Newspapers were still thriving. The news just got to the editor's desk faster.

Then came the Internet, along with its ability to transform at the highest level whatever it happens to touch. The Internet didn't merely change the print newspaper; it actually eroded its viability as a commercial undertaking. And although the personal computer made travel agents more efficient, the Internet rendered them unnecessary for much of the travel we do.

The reason for all this transformation is information efficiency. The Internet enables businesses to replace physical infrastructure with virtual infrastructure. Google News employs no reporters; it borrows them. It uses no paper; it prints its stories on the screen. It doesn't need paperboys to carry the load. It uses data pipes and TCP/IP instead.

The more information intensive a business is, the more likely it is to be affected by powerful new forms of information efficiency, and the more likely it will be to change its form. Just look at what the Internet has done to retail shopping. Nothing virtual can replace the physical act of window shopping along Rome's opulent Via del Corso. Many people go there not so much to find out what Ferragamo's spring collection looks like as to mingle with crowds from around the world that flock there for the experience, every bit as much as they feel a need to stand beneath the dome inside St. Peter's Basilica.

But if you have a regular need for, say, the same type of printer cartridge, there is no need to get in the car on a hot day, drive several miles, and try to find a spot in the parking lot at Office Depot. Not only can you order your cartridge from Amazon.com, a bottomless pit of "in stock" items, but also you're likely to pay less and save yourself the sales tax. In short, when a shopping experience is something you'd just as soon avoid, you're usually better off just firing up your browser.

Advertising has also undergone a wholesale change, thanks in large part to the Internet. At the end of the day, advertising is really about getting information to consumers and changing their behavior in the process, and a medium as powerful and ubiquitous as the Internet is at least as likely to make that happen as is a newspaper or a television set. Google certainly figured that out, and the company's search-based advertising has been a huge success.

Stock trading, another information-intensive business, is very different now because of the Internet. Were it not for the Internet, day traders wouldn't exist. And now Wall Street has grown increasingly dominated by high-frequency trading, where powerful computers deploy algorithms that execute thousands of orders every second. And where does the information that feeds those algorithms come from? The Internet, of course. Computers scan dozens of public and private marketplaces simultaneously and spot trends and shifting strategies before other investors can so much as blink. Big Wall Street firms such as Goldman Sachs can afford to spend the money on hypertrading technology, and many investors with no access to hypertrading are crying foul. But in the end, it's the hypertraders who have, in true Darwinian fashion, adapted to a supercharged, Internet-driven trading environment—and are reaping the rewards.

By contrast, businesses that depend on physical forms of infrastructure will carry on much as they have for years, and the Internet will have relatively little effect on the way they operate. The plumber will still have to come to your home to fix a broken pipe. True, he might have to promote his business on the Web instead of in the Yellow Pages; his customers may vet him first by checking recommendations on the Internet; his billing system may be different in the future. Nevertheless, he'll still have to make house calls. The way restaurants interact with the world is changing: many use online services like OpenTable, for their reservation systems, while others order food and supplies from vendors over the Internet. But they will still have kitchens and deliver food to tables. People will continue to go to Starbucks to meet friends and drink lattes. And while sports fans may buy their tickets online, they will still want to attend baseball and football games in person.

Another category of businesses involves those that live and die based on how well they physically deliver goods and services but whose delivery infrastructure is expensive and can be improved with the help of the Internet. FedEx and UPS will always have to deliver the goods on time, but the routing of their trucks and the tracking of packages en route can be made much more efficient through the use of the Internet. To the outsider's eye, automotive and computer manufacturers appear relatively unchanged, but their internal operations have been transformed by the Internet.

Dell Inc. is a good example of a company that was able to take advantage of a changed environment by integrating its own operations with suppliers using Information-Age tools. Perhaps you've ordered a PC from Dell, a manufacturing company with almost no factory at all. You probably placed your order online and never stepped foot in a Best Buy or CompUSA. For a long time, Dell sold its computers directly to customers over the Internet and used no retail outlets at all.

At the top of its game in the late 1990s, Dell was an enviable model of efficiency. The company carried almost no inventory. It billed customers' credit cards for purchases instantly and took its time paying suppliers, which enabled the company to use the cash float to finance its operations. It would have been impossible for Dell to run this type of operation without the Internet. Dell outsourced the manufacturing of all the components for its systems; then, once customer orders came in, it assembled these components into final systems at its plant near Austin, Texas.

Most of the components came from Asia, and for Dell to run its operation smoothly, it had to know at all times where in the supply chain materials could be found. It was imperative that the components arrived just in time, so that Dell would always have what was needed to put together systems in a few days and ship them to customers. At the same time, the company had to be capable of modifying its own production schedule and those of its suppliers at a moment's notice so that supply would always match demand.

Dell exerted a level of control over its operations that Henry Ford could have only dreamed about in the 1920's, when he built automobiles at his famous River Rouge manufacturing plant. This complex would eventually become the most famous of American auto factories, covering more than two square miles and comprising a power plant, an ore-processing facility, docks, and one hundred miles of interior railroad tracks. Iron ore and coal were transformed on-site into engine blocks. In fact, the Rouge became a model of vertical integration: raw material entered one door and new automobiles exited the other.

To run a complex manufacturing process, with hundreds of part types to be assembled and thousands of workers and machining operations to be scheduled, adds up to a logistical nightmare. To do it effectively, you have to know what is going on at hundreds of locations within a factory. One of the reasons Ford built the complex was his desire to know at any given time what was going on at every stage of the production process.

Those unfamiliar with manufacturing would find it difficult to understand how complex the process is. Having a plant report to me when I was at Intel was a real eye-opener. Of course, my experience predates just-in-time systems and the rise in quality standards that came with them. Machines would break down and cause parts to pile up. Suppliers would ship parts too early and too late, and when they did arrive they often didn't work or were in the wrong quantity. Inventory was constantly being moved in and out of storerooms in amounts that couldn't be kept track of accurately.

Now we have the Internet, which makes keeping track of things on the factory floor much easier, whether the plant is behind one's office or thousands of miles away. Henry Ford undoubtedly ran a better manufacturing system than I did, but the challenge of having to use manual systems to collect data from numerous points in a manufacturing system spread over two square miles must have been considerable. Dell, using the Internet, has better knowledge of what is going on with suppliers six thousand miles away than Ford had of what was happening under his one huge roof. Because of the Internet, Dell hardly needs a factory at all.

As I've said repeatedly, things happen quickly in this new world. Dell's business strategy is already under attack. Dell's former position as the world's largest PC manufacturer has been taken over by Hewlett-Packard, which took the Dell strategy one step further and moved large parts of its operation to China. Adopting a different business model from Dell's, Hewlett-Packard now hires low-cost Asian factories to build complete systems. By doing so it obviates the need to establish higher-cost assembly plants in the U.S. Dell, in the meantime, has lost its low-cost edge.

Many businesses are changing in similar ways. The days when all their operations had to be under one roof to be coordinated are long gone. The most successful will gain access to the finest talent and the most favorable cost structure wherever they are situated.

One downside of this process is the disappearance of good jobs, which the Internet has accelerated in a number of ways, among them by making it relatively painless for businesses to exploit differences in labor costs. This was obviously not always the case. When I worked for Intel, we shipped semiconductor chips to the Philippines, Malaysia, and Barbados for assembly—a process that could take weeks. We couldn't help but feel a loss of control whenever the chips left the Intel plant in Santa Clara. Today, because companies can seamlessly plug workers in a developing country into an integrated manufacturing process in Europe or the United States, they can instantly take advantage of any differences in costs and move production to the cheapest locations. Information on the Internet not only makes this possible but also enables them to find parts, keep track of their movement, respond to changing demand for them, redesign them when necessary, and instantly transmit design changes to product engineers almost anywhere. With the job market depending less on geography, the less advantaged lose out.

Information-intensive jobs are particularly vulnerable. We have all called a local company for help and had the call answered in good but heavily accented English by somebody in India or the Philippines.

(Often enough now, the accents are less heavy as support companies begin to train the speech of those answering the phones.) This outsourcing of customer service is possible because records can be transferred over the Internet so inexpensively.

But the ease of transferring records doesn't mean that only low-skilled, low-wage jobs can be outsourced. Medical images can be sent electronically to developing countries, where skilled radiologists can make diagnoses. In 2006, as a cost-reduction measure, a medical practice in Singapore began transmitting X-rays over the Internet to a company in Bangalore, India, called Teleradiology Solutions. Teleradiology now has dozens of customers in the U.S. as well. Results for routine X-rays come back the same day, and emergency reports are provided within thirty minutes. And because it is so simple to send engineering documentation around the world, companies have begun to use programmers in Russia, the Baltic countries, and India to write software and to design semiconductors. Some companies use design teams spread around the world, each in a different time zone, so that work can proceed twenty-four hours a day.

On a trip in November 2007 to India, I visited an outsourcing company that was doing work for Lehman Brothers, the investment bank, which began its outsourcing program in 2002 with a goal of cutting costs 50 percent by going to round-the-clock operations, gaining access to a trained labor pool, and, as one Lehman executive put it, freeing up "important resources for more value-added work." The initial effort focused on sending offshore the more mundane work, such as simple software and help-desk operations. While on the trip I visited one of Lehman's outsourcing partners in Mumbai. When I arrived, I thought that, at most, the outsourcing would consist of market analysis or accounting. But I soon discovered that the Indian contractor was performing due diligence on financial offerings that Lehman planned to market to investors. I was blown away. I had thought this to be one of the fundamental jobs of Wall Street bankers and a significant part of the unique value that investment banks offered to their customers. I had also assumed that in order to do a creditable job you had to be in intimate contact with the market and the company being scrutinized. But no one in India had met anyone involved in the business or stepped foot in the U.S.; yet these people were providing Lehman with the very analysis that trained experts in New York should have been doing. I felt that I was looking at the Wall Street version of Milli Vanilli, the pop group that in 1990 earned a Grammy for the Best New Artist only to have its success turn to infamy when it was discovered that the group members were lip-synching and that the actual recorded voices did not belong to the artists. I could not help but wonder whether hedge funds would have fought to buy Lehman's high-yield offerings if they knew the words in the offering memorandum were just well-packaged lip-synching.

Outsourcing isn't just an international phenomenon. American companies were doing it nationally long before many of the jobs were sent overseas. The most remarkable example I've ever come across involved the U.S. Postal Service and its automated mail-sorting systems. In the 1990s, post office executives decided that in places where labor costs were high, when a machine was unable to read a zip code, instead of having a local postal worker sit there deciphering the numbers a more cost-effective solution would be to send a video image of the zip code somewhere else, where hourly wages were lower, and have a worker do the job there.

When information can be moved accurately, inexpensively, and quickly, and when products can be shipped reliably by air, ship, and train, businesses have the ability to take advantage of the smallest cost differences. And that is precisely what businesses do. Some may not want to, preferring to keep the factories running locally, but they have little choice but to lower their costs. If they don't, some competitor will, and may well drive them out of business.

Positive feedback kicks in with offshoring. If some companies start to move operations offshore to save costs, then others are compelled to do the same. The more companies that do it, the greater the pressure on other companies to follow suit. The process continues until there is very little left to send offshore. At each step of the way, the Internet is facilitating the process by making that process easier and more efficient.

Basically what the Internet does is connect rapidly responding businesses with slow-responding environments. Systems engineers don't like to make these types of connections because it can drive things to extremes before they can be corrected. For example, a country might lose all of its high-paying electronics-manufacturing jobs because labor costs are much lower in developing countries. It might take decades for the wages in a developing country to rise. Although businesses are often quick to respond to changing conditions, wages, currency valuations, and government policies move slowly.

Ideally, wages in developing countries should rise as demand for their workers increases. In Bangalore, wages have risen sharply in recent years, as the great technical talent that was once abundant there is now in short supply. Bangalore engineers are continually seizing new opportunities and switching jobs. This has, in turn, made offshoring to Bangalore less attractive. But Bangalore is an exception, not the rule. In most developing countries, where there remains an abundance of less skilled labor, wages, benefits, working conditions, and on-the-job safety can take decades to improve. And, particularly in today's fast-changing world, a decade is an eternity. So for businesses in developed countries, offshoring remains an attractive solution. At the same time, however, social conditions in those developed countries, where jobs have disappeared, tend to be disrupted.

Much of our thinking about free trade was formed at a time when countries lived in relative isolation. Far fewer developed countries' economies were subject to offshore opportunities. Because moving manufacturing jobs out of a country was so complex, for a long time it made little sense to do so. But along with the coming of the Internet, the education level in many developing countries has improved, in addition to the fact that many engineers who came to the United

States to get educated are now returning home for jobs. This movement, combined with the frictionless system the Internet has created, has made foreign labor pools more available and attractive.

While it once appeared that a lot of jobs would remain safe, now, unless a product or service must be delivered locally, almost no jobs are safe. Apropos of this local issue, workers in Asia would find it hard to build a rapid transit system in Chicago or repair a bridge in Minneapolis. A waiter in Mumbai can't serve me curry at my favorite Indian restaurant in Palo Alto. If I end up in a hospital with a heart attack, the nurses who care for me have to be present. Still, it's amazing how many jobs can be performed remotely as a result of information efficiency.

When I was with Intel we had a design center in Tel Aviv that produced sophisticated circuits. Because it was so difficult in the 1970s to make such arrangements work smoothly, few companies even tried. The long midnight phone calls made the job of coordinating painful. Today, with the Internet and videoconferencing, much of the friction has been removed from the system. Even small start-up companies have the ability to access talent in India and Eastern Europe.

Few industries are as information intensive as the newspaper business. Since the appearance of the first American newspaper, the *Public Occurrence,* in Boston in 1690, followed a few decades later by *The Boston News-Letter,* printed newspapers and the information they convey have served as both mainstay and lifeblood of a democratic society. Newspapers provided what the historian Henry Steel Commager once called "the raw material of history." What imbued them with such gravitas was in part their very physical nature—the heavy black type, the heft of the paper itself, the high stacks of them on street corners, all of which commanded our attention.

The rise of the Internet changed all of that. It caused a seismic shift, not just in the way information is delivered but in the way people look for their news in the first place. Executives at the helm of big, lumbering, deeply entrenched newspapers have had tremendous trouble adjusting, which has made their newspapers ripe for extinction. Circulation has declined, advertising revenue has plummeted, and news holes have shrunk. Craigslist has snatched the classified advertising base. Denver, Seattle, and Tucson have now only one daily print newspaper, and San Francisco may become the first major city without one. A battalion of blogs has captured many former newspaper readers. Meanwhile, Google is serving up headlines and providing news stories around the world and not charging for subscriptions. In so doing, Google is using stories the newspapers' own reporters have written. Meanwhile, the papers' reporting staffs are being cut to the bone. As a friend of mine is fond of saying, the papers are saving their buildings by sacrificing their brains.

Information efficiency is at work in the newspaper world. Paper is being replaced by bits and bytes. When most people think about the physical nature of newspapers, they tend to focus on the things they can see and touch. They worry about the trees that are cut down and the paper that has to be recycled. It is hard to conceive of how physical the newspaper process is until one looks inside the building where a paper is produced. I remember my excitement as a small boy visiting a newspaper facility. There were the giant presses fed by large rolls of paper that had to be loaded onto the press with forklifts. Paper raced through the presses. The technology seemed overwhelming. Typesetters worked at Mergenthaler Linotype machines that cast lead bars of hot type. The bars were then set in frames as pages were composed. Then the presses rolled, all at great cost to the publisher.

In the 1920s, my father purchased the Berkshire News Agency in Reading, Pennsylvania, from the Annenberg family. The agency used to distribute daily and Sunday newspapers from Philadelphia and New York into the Reading market. In the 1950s, when I was in my teens, I went back to Reading to learn the business. I remember vividly how on weekends, when big trucks would roll in from the big cities, I would help unload them and then manually stuff the Sunday papers with special supplements and advertising sections. Early the next morning we would load the papers on our smaller trucks to be distributed to newsstands that sold them and paperboys who delivered them.

Every time I pass a newsstand I think of those hours of tedious late-night and early-morning work at the news agency. Then my mind turns to the massive rolls of paper, the whirring press, and the hot type machines. With online news, all of that goes away; a physical distribution system is not required—no newsstands, delivery trucks, or newspaper boys riding bicycles. No presses, and no massive rolls of paper. This subtraction means that you can become a newspaper substitute with a very small investment. Information efficiency has powered the rise of the blogger and, in several cities, nonprofit professional journalism.

Newspapers will not go away entirely. But they will decline in importance and influence. And their form will change. Many of the surviving papers will start to deliver their content in electronic form only. A great many of their readers will end up reading blogs tailored to their particular interests and political proclivities. More and more citizen journalists will furnish us with news and opinions, as well as misinformation and rumors.

In San Diego, New Haven, the Twin Cities, Seattle, St. Louis, and Chicago, professional journalists have banded together and formed nonprofit organizations to offer quality investigative reporting to their communities. The VoiceofSanDiego.org has exposed government conflicts of interest, secret pay raises that ought to have been public, corruption in the realm of low-income housing, and the reporting of misleading crime statistics. While the nonprofit business model may not prove successful in the long run, if it does it will be because of information efficiency, which has reduced the cost of publishing a newspaper. By doing away with the physical infrastructure of paper, ink, printing presses, and newsrooms, running a newspaper can be pretty cheap. At the same time, good journalism is expensive, and the quality of the reporting could suffer if news organizations don't invest in experienced reporters.

In the age of the Internet there are newer jobs, but also fewer jobs. The recording industry has always been protected by copyright laws, but what really made it practicable were the inconvenience and cost of copying music and the difficulty of distributing those copies. Before the invention of magnetic tape, vinyl records made it virtually impossible to copy a recording. The development of tape cassettes solved that issue. But, fortunately for the recording companies, it took as long to record one cassette as it did to play the music. Enter the Internet, which made it not only easy and cheap to copy music, but also simple and fast to distribute the copies.

Recordings have moved from phonographs, tape decks, and CD players to iPods and MP3 players. And the Internet has become a major means of promoting and distributing music. In the process, the pricing structure of the recording industry has been destroyed. Consumers no longer have to purchase an album for $14.95 to get a copy of one song they want. In some respects, we have returned to the 1950s, when consumers purchased recordings of single songs on 45-rpm records for 89 cents—an inflation-adjusted price of about $7 in today's dollars. Instead of going to a store to buy small records with big holes in the center, we can sit at home and download single songs to our iPods for 99 cents.

One reason the price of downloads has to be kept so low is that if it were too high consumers would just download illegal copies. The effect of all this new technology has been the restructuring of the distribution system for recorded music. Fewer and fewer physical media are sold. Retail stores are being driven out of existence.

In 2003, Wherehouse Entertainment, a chain of music retail stores, filed for Chapter 11 bankruptcy, blaming illegal downloading for its predicament. In 2004 and again in 2006, Tower Records declared bankruptcy as well. In the wake of these failures and the success of the iPod, the major record labels started a frantic quest for viable strategies for selling music downloads. They were trapped in the distribution paradigm of the past, concerned about selling music directly over the Internet to customers and thus cutting out the retailers, which still accounted for a large share of their business. Equally troubling were illegal downloads. Even though legal ones are now available from Apple's iTunes store and a number of other companies, illegal copying continues to flourish.

You might even question whether there is a role for the recording industry in the future. And you would not be alone. The reason recording companies existed was to find artists, promote them and their works, produce recordings, and get recordings into distribution. For most musicians, the sale of recordings has never generated much revenue. The recordings were intended to promote the artists, who then earned their living by selling tickets to live performances.

Now, with physical album sales declining at a steady clip, and sales of individual digital tracks rising, the structure of the music business is radically changing. Some well-known musicians and their managers are sidestepping the recording industry altogether. Brian Message, manager of the alternative band Radiohead, which started giving away entire albums on the Internet in 2009, started a venture that same year called Polyphonic, to invest a few hundred thousand dollars in new and rising artists who were not signed to record deals, and then help them create their own direct links to audiences over the Internet.

Such ventures signal deep shifts in the music business. The major labels—Sony Music, Warner Music, EMI, and Universal Music—no longer have a firm grip on creating and selling professional music and producing hits with prime placement on the radio.

Dallas Green is a good example. The musician (not to be confused with the former major league baseball player and manager) promotes himself under the name City and Colour. He has a major presence on MySpace, where many recording artists hang out. Selections of

Green's music can be listened to for free on the site. And by all indications, the strategy works. Those samples have been played more than ten million times. Green promotes his upcoming shows on the site. His recordings can be purchased as downloads from iTunes and mymerchtable.com. A company called Vagrant Records distributes his CDs. Green spends a lot of time communicating with his fans over the Internet. He depends on his music going viral (spread by word of mouth, e-mail, and blogs) to build his fan base.

Digitally recorded music is just a string of bits. The principle of information efficiency should apply quite broadly to such a product. Move the bits, and you don't need physical media, you don't need physical distribution, and you may not even need the recording studios. Clearly the recording industry is losing power in this new environment. Artists like Dallas Green are increasingly in charge of their own destinies. They have ways to interact directly with their own fans. Their fans have been empowered by the Internet. Green's fans can send his songs to friends and help build the ranks of his followers. So one has to wonder whether the recording industry is going to become marginal, possibly as irrelevant as print newspapers and travel agents.

TWELVE

How Overconnectivity
Stole Your Privacy

The loss of privacy is a perfect example of the troubles that can arise in an Internet-powered environment. Even before the Internet, companies had been able to assemble very large customer databases that could be searched and used for marketing and credit checking. And identity theft certainly existed, though on a much smaller scale.

Many of us don't want much information about us floating around on the Internet, and we're unsettled by the idea of companies assembling massive dossiers about where and how we live. And as our assets, and information about those assets, continue to move from physical to virtual space, the environment we increasingly occupy is more accident-prone than ever, and the potential for identity theft only grows.

The Internet, in this case, has been the ultimate turbocharger. It made it cheaper and easier to build massive files and to correlate information, and the amassing of that information happened quickly—too quickly for the government to respond. Lax security on the Internet has made it harder to design theft-proof systems and easier for cyberthieves to evade detection.

This is where information efficiency comes into play. In the 1980s, the size of databases was constrained by the cost of collecting and storing their contents, much of which had to be manually transcribed. Although information from a credit card could be collected at a cash register, the data were stored in isolated computer systems, or offline on large magnetic tapes, or on discs that had to be mounted on a system before their lists could be used. So if you were a marketing company and wanted to buy, say, a subscriber list from a magazine, it would be shipped to you in physical form, either as a computer printout or on magnetic tape. Not only was storing the lists difficult, but merging them (e.g., to find out if a *Sports Illustrated* subscriber also shopped at Walmart) was close to impossible. And such lists were rarely, if ever, stolen.

The arrival of the Internet changed everything. Suddenly it was possible to send, retrieve, and store information easily. At the same time, the physical constraints that secured it were now gone. What's more, the value of information could be compounded. That is, isolated bits of data aren't worth very much. For example, if I know only your telephone number or address or sex, each datum isn't worth much. But if I can put these three things about you together, the information has greater value. And if I know all this plus your income, the magazines you subscribe to, where you shop on the Internet, and what you buy in the mall, as well as the type of car you own, then the information becomes substantially more valuable. One might call it value by association.

Once the Internet entered the picture, the practice of data mining, as it is known, became a perfect positive feedback situation. First, the cost of capturing the data declined, because information about transactions can be gathered—with no human effort—whenever someone shops on the Internet or checks out at a store using a credit card. Second, the cost of information processing dropped precipitously, so that mining data for results became very cheap. And, of course, the cost of storing data declined steeply as well.

Companies selling consumer information can now make big profits. Information about customers was always valuable. But because more data are available now, marketers can target their potential customers more precisely. Last, but in no way least, the value of a product increases as its potential market grows. This in turn creates a virtuous circle. As a company acquires more data, the value of its product increases, enabling it to acquire still more customers and to reduce the cost of building its market share.

ChoicePoint, the data aggregation company, is one of the best examples of the way adding relevant databases can increase the value of service and, hence, the size of a business. The company started in 1997 as a spin-off from Equifax, one of the three major credit bureaus. ChoicePoint's strategy was to make the country a safer place by providing a comprehensive and trusted source for background checks. One of its goals was to ease the way for employers to determine if prospective employees had criminal records. There is no doubt it has been effective. Five million searches by its customers turned up close to four hundred thousand applicants who had prior criminal records—information any potential employer would certainly like to have.

Soon after its start, ChoicePoint went on an acquisition binge. Within seven years, it had purchased more than fifty companies, whose databases were added to the mix, making background checks more reliable. As ChoicePoint swallowed more databases, the value of its searches rose and the number of clients served grew from one thousand to more than fifty thousand.

Today, the company, which is one of the major suppliers of personal information to law enforcement authorities and business firms, has more than 250 terabytes of data on more than two hundred million individuals. That's more than a megabyte—or four hundred pages—per person. Databases about our lives truly represent the unregulated Wild West. Most disturbing, it is an accident-prone environment subject to abuse. We read endless stories about laptops containing thousands of records being lost or stolen, databases being accessed by hackers, and information being used in shady marketing practices to swindle the naïve and the elderly.

Today you can buy a list of 3.3 million "Elderly Opportunity

Seekers," older people looking for ways to make money, 4.7 million "Suffering Seniors," people with cancer or Alzheimer's disease, or 500,000 gamblers over 55, for 8.5 cents per person. As one list dealer said in its online advertisement: "These people are gullible. They want to believe that their luck can change." Thieves working in India and using such lists focused their efforts on old Army veterans and bilked them out of thousands of dollars by posing as government workers updating files.

While reading about all the accidents occurring in the personal database world, I began to think back to the warnings of Charles Perrow, the accident theorist. He argued that some systems, such as nuclear power plants, should never be built because there was no way to make them safe enough and the consequences of a failure were so terrible. I began to wonder if personal database systems fell into this category.

Then there are database thieves. In 2006, Scott Levine was convicted of stealing 1.6 billion records by performing 137 searches of the Acxiom database in 2003. He had been the head of Snipermail.com and knew how to exploit weak access controls. He used the stolen data to increase the size of Snipermail's own database and make it a more attractive acquisition target. Levine used just one of numerous access points. To make a system really secure, all entries have to be well controlled. That's why jails don't have a lot of doors.

Credit bureaus, such as Equifax, have histories of millions of customers. ChoicePoint, Seisint, and Acxiom have billions of records containing addresses; phone, credit card, Social Security, and driver's license numbers; criminal records; employment histories; and marketing information, including the products individuals buy—all of which can be aggregated to create detailed profiles of consumers. This information is, in turn, available for sale to law enforcement agencies, catalog retailers, and companies that want to find customers.

The information sold by Equifax, ChoicePoint, Seisint, and Acxiom is safe as long as it is protected not only by these companies but also by every business that purchases it. Unfortunately, customers have very different levels of security, some being diligent, others less so, and many simply naïve when it comes to security issues. Sometimes large amounts of data are stored on a single site that can be accessed from anywhere in the world. This means it is vulnerable to attack from numerous quarters. When data were stored in physical form, you had to be somewhere specific to steal it. Now you can be anywhere—the Internet doesn't discriminate. Obviously, this accessibility raises the number of potential thieves as well.

Some identity thefts are the result of simple error. An occasional mistake by a small online retailer is understandable. What is disturbing, however, is errors at huge and sophisticated companies that ought to be secure. For example, in February 2005 the Bank of America reported that it had lost computer tapes containing the names, addresses, and credit card and social security numbers of some 1.2 million federal employees The tapes were probably stolen from a commercial plane by baggage handlers.

One of the most disconcerting thefts involved ChoicePoint. In 2005, nearly 145,000 consumer records containing sensitive information were sold to a bogus business the company had not vetted adequately. According to Robert O'Harrow in his book *No Place to Hide* (Free Press, 2005), ChoicePoint became accident-prone because it lacked a policy to ensure that information was sold only in situations "where there is a specific consumer-driven transaction or benefit" or law enforcement purpose. Indeed, not until after the theft did the company hire a chief privacy officer to help verify the credentials of its customers.

So, keeping your identity safe now depends on the honesty and reliability of those ChoicePoint customers who purchased the lists, as well as their ability to keep these records secure from thieves anxious to steal them. As a result, if ChoicePoint wants to guarantee the security of its data it must in turn rely on the security of numerous other systems. Realistically, the chance of complete invulnerability is zero.

In short, the rapid change in the environment powered by the Internet has taken us to a place most of us would prefer not to be. Current regulations are not adequate to protect us. And the system is evolving so quickly that it is hard to see how the regulators will ever catch up. Meanwhile, the skills of the invaders are improving, and their numbers are increasing as the richness of the territory builds. There are, of course, numerous remedies. For example, credit-reporting agencies will block your records, for a fee. Anyone who wishes access to a consumer's records must get a password from the consumer. This obviously makes it more difficult to gain access to such information. If the default state for credit records was a blocked one, the ease of stealing identities would be greatly reduced but so would the income of companies such as Equifax, Experian, and Transunion.

We should consider applying to ChoicePoint and other data aggregators the same rules that control the U.S. government's collection of personal data as legislated in the 1974 Privacy Act. As Robert O'Harrow, the investigative journalist, has pointed out, the act prohibited the government from building databases of dossiers "unless the information about individuals was directly relevant to an agency's mission." However, no such restrictions apply to private companies such as ChoicePoint, which are only too happy to perform such services for the government. By outsourcing the collecting of personal information, the government doesn't have to ensure the data are accurate, or be required to correct data, as it would be under the Privacy Act. "This limitation to the Privacy Act is critical," O'Harrow wrote. "It allows [data brokers like ChoicePoint] to amass huge databases that the government is legally prohibited from creating."

Contagions, as we know, are spread through interconnections. And there is no medium for interconnection quite like the Internet for helping them flourish. It is inexpensive and fast. And, unlike conventional media, it enables participants to listen and speak, making them feel more a part of things. I saw what this did to my Rambus stock on the Yahoo! message board. And I saw the sense of community created by the Whole Earth 'Lectronic Link, known simply as the WELL. Created in 1985, the WELL was one of the first virtual communities. Although it never grew huge in numbers, the WELL's influence was extraordinary. The site comprised mostly discussions of topics ranging from serious politics to trivia. For years, long before the Internet took hold, WELL members lived, loved, and grieved together, although many of them had never met in person.

Today, people of all ages go online to communicate and commiserate, making the Internet an ideal medium for supporting and intensifying thought contagions. Of course, like anything else about the Internet, there are two schools of thought on this communication feature. Some believe that by providing access to diverse points of view the Internet can help dissipate thought contagions, the hope being that if people are exposed to divergent opinions, they will become more sympathetic to those views. Others believe just the opposite—that the Internet serves to polarize views. I suspect both positions are valid, but I lean toward the outlook that the Internet drives opinions to extremes.

Consider that research has found that the number of hate groups in the United States has grown rapidly since the 9/11 attacks on the World Trade Center. Experts hold that the Internet is the primary factor in this increase. Although hate groups have hitherto used conventional media to communicate with their members and attract new ones, the Internet has provided them with audiences. For example, the likes of white supremacists have historically been isolated in various communities. The Internet has made it easier for them to contact one another, reinforce their beliefs, and add to the power of their movement.

Thought contagions are driven by positive feedback processes. The key to initiating and sustaining them is the ability to recruit new participants. For a contagion to exist, at least one new member must be added for every one lost. The Internet is an ideal vehicle for supporting this positive feedback process.

Since the Internet's reach is global, the number of people an idea can reach for a minimal cost is very large. For one thing, potential believers can find like-minded groups just by doing a simple Internet search. For another, once people meet in virtual space, the Internet provides valuable data, in the form of text and images that can reinforce the idea. Finally, the Internet can be used to organize remote groups to recruit new believers.

The Internet is a wonderful medium for creating a feeling of belonging, just as the WELL did with its members. People can meet one another in virtual space, communicate one-to-many on blogs, and form one-on-one relationships.

Some thought contagions burst on the scene, grow rapidly, peak, and peter out. The hula hoop craze lasted from January to October 1958 and then fizzled. During those nine wild months, Wham-O sold more than one hundred million hoops. Political contagions usually build more slowly and last longer.

We have long known that people gravitate to parts of the media that reinforce their beliefs. Liberals listen to NPR; conservatives tune in to Rush Limbaugh and Fox News. We also know that being in like-minded company tends to grow and harden preexisting biases.

In his blog Rough Type, Nicholas G. Carr, a writer on information technology, has discussed a phenomenon studied extensively by network theorists, namely, the tendency for slight biases to lead to segregation. For example, the desire of people not to be part of an extreme minority quickly leads to segregated neighborhoods. Carr made the following observation:

> In the real world, with its mortgages and schools and jobs and moving vans, the "mechanical forces" of segregation move fairly slowly; there are brakes on the speed with which we pull up stakes and change where we live. In internet commu-

nities, there are no such constraints. Making a community-defining decision is as simple as clicking on a link—adding a feed to your blog reader, say, or a friend to your social network. Given the presence of a slight bias to be connected to people similar to ourselves, the segregation effect would thus tend to happen much faster—and with even more extreme consequences—on the internet.

In other words, the Internet promotes thought contagions. Let's return to the white supremacists' use of the Internet, where, because little expense is involved, their Web sites have proliferated dramatically and recruitment now mostly takes place. For a while, neo-Nazi groups found it convenient to use Facebook to spread their ideology, until Facebook kicked them off. Stormfront.org, whose slogan is "White Pride Worldwide," is packed with hateful, prejudiced blogs describing how to plant ideas in the minds of new recruits. Moreover, the Internet gives these groups a platform for preaching their ideology anonymously.

Of course, good thought contagions as well as destructive ones can be spread by the Internet. Political campaigns are all about thought contagions. Whether you believe them good or bad depends on your political persuasion. In the past, the political parties have used conventional media and various tried-and-true techniques to spread their ideas—speeches, conventions, door-to-door campaigns, direct mail, radio, and television. Barack Obama has taught the world how to use the Internet to spread political ideas.

The Internet is affecting almost everything we do and nearly every aspect of our lives. We can take advantage of its benefits and beware of its dangers. The key challenge will be to recognize the potential outcomes, guard against the threats, and, when something good seems possible from a positive feedback process, get out of the way.

THIRTEEN

Everything Is Interconnected—Part I

Anything in isolation, like a single atom, is interesting enough. But link a few atoms to one another and things get exciting. Connect carbon, nitrogen, and hydrogen to form the four nucleotides—adenine, guanine, thymine, and cytosine—then connect those nucleotides with chains of deoxyribose and you get DNA. Connect layer upon layer of DNA and you get life.

And from life comes civilizations, which require interconnections in order to thrive. To develop culturally and technologically, citizens have to be productive; this productivity in turn requires specialization. But if someone specializes—by making, let's say, wheels—he has to engage in trade to satisfy his other needs. In ancient times when large groups of people congregated in and around cities, some farmed while others gathered wood or made tools. Still others made clothing. They met in the city's marketplace and traded one service or product for another. From those densely connected environments came organized hierarchies—businesses, temples of religious order, and armies. Large concentrations of interconnected people made possible support of the arts. Over time, civilization emerged.

Many forms of interconnection carry information: radio, television, telephones, books, and the news media. Each is deeply intertwined with other, physical forms of connectivity, such as airplanes, trains, and ships. There are also less obvious forms of connectivity.

Belief systems, for instance, are one very powerful form. They promote social and religious behavior. Of course, belief systems could not exist without information interconnections to spread those beliefs. But once a belief system is in place, transferring only a little bit of information over the Internet can trigger powerful responses. Just one example is the reaction of Muslim communities around the world to the publication in 2005 of provocative cartoons of Muhammad.

Dependencies created by nature are another powerful form of connectivity. Nothing illustrates this better than water. Southern California is dependent on water from the Colorado River and on water drawn from the Sacramento–San Joaquin delta. Persistent tensions exist between environmentalists, who want to save the salmon and other endangered species in the delta, and farmers in the southern part of the state, who rely on its water for their livelihood. Iraq and Syria are tightly linked to Turkey through their dependence on water from the Tigris. Iraqi and Syrian officials are concerned that Turkey's construction of the massive Ilisu Dam will reduce the quality and volume of water flowing into Iraq. A deeper concern is that Turkey will be able to shut off the flow to both countries. The project has been opposed by a collection of odd bedfellows—not just the governments of both Syria and Iraq, but preservationists, archaeologists, and Kurdish populations in Turkey that would be displaced by the dam.

Oil is another connection that has created some unlikely alliances. Our dependence on oil connects us with oil-rich countries—Venezuela, Nigeria, Iraq, Saudi Arabia. The development of supertankers and pipelines has made it much less expensive to transport oil from those distant locations and increased our dependence on foreign oil. If the cost of transportation was very high, I have no doubt we would be driving more fuel-efficient cars today.

I am amazed at how frequently I encounter the words "connected" and "interconnected"—in newspapers, on blogs, in casual conversation. When people use these words, they are talking about infrastructure without really understanding what it does. This shortsightedness is like pointing to a building without understanding that if strong steel beams didn't hold the building up it would fall down. The key point is that anytime you create a heavily interconnected environment that links together active elements, there is a chance of creating positive feedback, driving rapid change, having accidents, and spreading contagions. The greater the number of interconnections, and the stronger they are, the more likely these dangers will exist. It doesn't matter whether the interconnection device relates to foreign debt, dependence on oil, or water from a distant source; whether to belief systems, railroads, telegraphs, generators on a power grid, or the subsidy of subprime mortgages, or, of course, whether it's hundreds of millions of computers, tablets, book readers, Web cameras, servers, or smart phones connected to the Internet. Each of these interconnections, whether weak or strong, has the potential to make systems more volatile.

Let's suppose for a minute that the Internet never came into existence, that in 1966 it never occurred to Bob Taylor to be annoyed by the fact that those three separate machines in his office at the Pentagon were unable to talk to one another. Let's imagine that Paul Baran never conjured up packet switching, that Larry Roberts never sketched what a distributed network might look like, and that Vint Cerf and Bob Kahn never wrote the paper that laid the foundation for TCP/IP. E-mail does not exist. Nor does instant messaging. There is no World Wide Web, and therefore no Amazon, no Google, no Facebook, and certainly no Twitter. All communications still take place in person, over the telephone, and by snail mail. Faxes and FedEx are as exotic as it gets. Now that we have purged the Internet from our brains, let us consider some situations that aren't merely Internet-free but instead driven by other forms of interconnectivity that we may not even think of as interconnectivity at all.

My reason for suggesting this imaginative leap is that I want you to understand that our society is filled with different types of interconnectivity and that these can have similar effects to those from Internet-powered interconnections.

There are hundreds of examples. One especially compelling "for-want-of-a-nail" story tells how the issuing of a few thousand German passports created an interconnection that helped bring the Soviet Union to its knees.

In the space of a few extraordinary months in 1989, the governments of East Germany, Bulgaria, Romania, and Czechoslovakia all collapsed. Soviet watchers around the world were astonished by the speed at which these radical changes occurred. In fact, the seeds for this rapid change had been sown for some time, owing in no small part to interconnections from the West into the East that fueled a diffusion of new knowledge in the form of democratic ideals, as well as a rewiring of the once-isolated, Soviet-controlled transportation system.

To appreciate fully the chain of events that led to the collapse, let's go back to the late 1940s. To increase control over Warsaw Pact countries, the Soviet government took actions to strengthen connections within the Soviet Union and its satellite states. It did this by greatly restricting commerce with the West and attempting to produce everything needed within the Soviet Union. At the same time, the Soviet government weakened connections beyond the Iron Curtain and in some cases eliminated them altogether.

During the 1950s, central planning had reduced dependence on foreign goods and produced excellent results. But as more and more peasants and women were absorbed into the workforce, to grow by adding more labor was no longer possible—the countries within the Soviet Union no longer had an abundance of workers. As a result, further economic development required importing new technology that would make workers more productive and exporting products to pay for it. This change required adopting world prices and moving toward market mechanisms. It was a strategy, however, that threatened the carefully crafted isolation of the Soviet Union, forcing openness and creating interconnections to the West, through which democratic influences were able to insinuate themselves and spread rapidly through the Soviet Bloc countries. Still, because of decades of continuous authoritarian rule, no one anticipated the serious repercussions that would occur. After all, Nicolae Ceausescu had managed to establish a personality cult in Romania, Erich Honecker continued to exert tight bureaucratic control over East Germany, and Wojciech Jaruzelski in 1981 had instituted martial law in Poland.

The apparent stability of these satellite governments made the Soviet government confident that it could move forward with much-needed reforms without negative consequences. So, in 1988, Soviet premier Mikhail Gorbachev announced his intention to remove some troops from Eastern Europe and indicated, at least tacitly, his support for the political and economic reforms occurring in Hungary. In the late 1980s, encouraged by Gorbachev's more liberal attitude, Hungary lifted most restrictions on travel to Austria. Although it had always been relatively easy for Soviet Bloc citizens to travel from satellite to satellite, none of these had allowed easy passage outside the Bloc. Also, it was relatively easy for East German citizens to obtain West German passports, not because East Germany encouraged it, but because West Germany considered all East Germans to be residents of the Federal Republic. To be issued a passport, East Germans needed only to show up at a West German embassy in Hungary, Poland, or Czechoslovakia and request one.

The passports, however, were useless for travel to the West, since none of the Soviet Bloc countries honored them. That all began to change on May 3, 1989, when Hungarian border guards began removing the barbed-wire fence on the Austrian border. In May 1989, the border between Hungary and Austria was officially opened, creating an interconnection between East and West. In September, the Hungarian government announced, over protests from the East German government, that it would allow all East Germans in the country to emigrate. By October, thirty-five thousand had left.

Suddenly West German passports that for years had been all but useless to East Germans became a ticket to freedom. In response to the border opening, West German embassies in the Soviet Bloc countries were deluged with requests for passports. The run on passports—fueled by a massive thought contagion—resembled a run on a failing bank. More than 3,000 East Germans crowded into the West German embassy in Prague. In an attempt to put the problem to rest, East German president Erich Honecker arranged to place the refugees on sealed trains and had them expelled from the East for "humanitarian reasons." The televised celebrations of the refugees' arrival in the West encouraged more and more East Germans to flock to the Prague embassy.

With positive feedback processes at work, it wasn't long before people throughout East Germany were making their grievances known. On November 4, five hundred thousand East Berliners marched the streets chanting slogans such as "We are one people." When news spread that permits would be granted promptly for private trips abroad, crowds began to gather at the Wall. Confused border guards, influenced by rumors about the new policy, permitted celebrating Easterners to pour across the checkpoints and scale the Wall. The night of November 9 marked the point of no return; people streamed across the border and took pickaxes to the wall. The collapse of the remaining governments soon followed.

Certainly the issuing of West German passports alone did not cause the collapse of the Soviet Union, just as the Internet did not cause the subprime debt crisis. But it did strengthen an interconnection—the transportation interconnection between Hungary and Austria. In some ways this is similar to the way the telegraph strengthened the rail interconnection for farmers in the nineteenth century or the way the Internet interconnection has facilitated free trade between nations. This connection to Austria was one of the key factors in getting the positive feedback process going that led to thought contagions ultimately producing half a million marchers in

East Berlin. When things are balanced on a knife edge, strengthening an interconnection can increase the feedback in the system and tip it over the edge into instability.

The few thousand passports served as what complex-system theorists call a butterfly effect—based on the idea that a butterfly flapping its wings in Asia can kick off a series of events that will lead to a hurricane in the Caribbean. The concept of the butterfly effect is especially instructive in that it shows how something small and easily dismissed can trigger a process with far-reaching consequences when positive feedback kicks in.

Everyone was surprised by the swift unfolding of events within the Soviet Bloc, just as we were by the 2008 financial crisis. And although the two incidents seem worlds apart, each is an example of how difficult it is to predict outcomes in a tightly connected, complex system.

Another example of the utter unpredictability of outcomes as a result of creating a connection without understanding where it might lead came into play two decades earlier, with Balinese rice farmers. In 1967, the Indonesian government, compelled by reports of agricultural breakthroughs elsewhere through the introduction of new seed varieties, chemical fertilizers, and pesticides, began providing "massive guidance" to Balinese farmers on how to adapt the "Green Revolution" to the growing of rice. At about the same time, the Asian Development Bank instituted a major irrigation project in Bali. To most agriculture experts, the decision of the Balinese to modernize their farming practices by planting new rice varieties and increasing yields seemed a sound and logical one. During the 1950s, Indonesia had imported nearly a million tons of rice a year in order to augment the country's own rice production and feed its population. The country's own output was significantly limited by a thousand-year-old agricultural system of cooperative water distribution and coordinated planting times that kept farmers from growing more than two crops a year, even though it was altogether feasible to grow three.

At the heart of this system was a mix of Hindu customs and rituals that involved frequent meetings at water temples, religious ceremonies, the worship of gods and goddesses who held sway over the earth and rivers, and reaching consensus among members of different castes. Aside from the blessings derived from these practices, for the system to work both upstream and downstream farmers had not only to agree to let their rice fields go fallow for a number of months every year, but also to do so at the same time. As a result of this coordinated planting-and-fallowing schedule, rice pests experienced an annual reduction in their habitat, and their populations were held in check. The ancient system put the brakes on a positive feedback process that would drive subsequent agricultural plagues.

As historically successful as they were, however, these traditional practices yielded to the spirit of the Green Revolution. By 1977, 70 percent of the rice fields in southcentral Bali had been planted with new varieties of rice. The government also encouraged triple-cropping, and the age-old practice of coordinating the fallowing of fields was largely abandoned. It was not long, however, before new pests emerged to attack the new varieties of rice. To counter one rice-eating pest, the brown plant-hopper, a new strain of rice called IR26 was introduced. When the tungro virus devastated the resulting crop, yet another variety was planted, only to be attacked by brown spot disease. Where crop losses from pests and disease were once as low as 1 percent, farmers were now—with continual cropping—experiencing losses as high as 50 percent. In the face of these failures, the government cut back on its "massive guidance" and began encouraging the Balinese farmers to return to their ancient water-temple system that had functioned so efficiently for hundreds of years—and whose limitations, it turned out, existed more in the minds of bureaucrats than in reality.

Governance by the traditional water-temple methods broke a very important interconnection between the agricultural pests and the crops. In doing so, it severed the positive feedback loop that supported the increase in pest populations. Letting the fields all go fallow at the same time cut off the pests' food supply, starving out the pest populations, whereas the seemingly advanced Green Revolution built a tight connection between the pests and their food supply, enabling the pests to multiply. Creating tight interconnections where none existed before can have surprising results.

There are, of course, hundreds of other examples. The automobile, for instance, is one of the most powerful interconnection technologies ever conceived and developed. It is another perfect example of unpredicted outcomes. As timely creations go, few were more ideally matched to the needs and geography of the United States than the automobile in the early twentieth century. It was a time when American cities were surrounded by vast areas of open space and plenty of oil was available to refine into gasoline. The automobile was also the ideal engine for America's economic growth through much of the century. Its mass production created thousands of factory jobs. It created markets for oil, steel, tires, glass, and machine tools. Service industries grew up to maintain, transport, finance, and insure automobiles.

The automobile also created a need for massive amounts of physical infrastructure—roads, bridges, homes in the suburbs, garages, and parking structures, all of which had to be built, fueling even more economic growth and changing the physical complexion of the United States more than any technological development that had come before, including the railroads.

Especially for people living in smog-plagued cities in the twenty-first century, it will no doubt come as a surprise to learn that the automobile was once viewed as a solution to urban pollution. But it indeed was. In New York City in the late 1800s, the stench of horse manure piles was awful. Flies, which were called the "queens of the dung heap," spread disease. Overworked horses died in their tracks, whipped by teamsters to pull heavy loads. Dead horses often clogged Broadway, and the disposal of the resulting offal polluted the bay. In 1880, the city removed fifteen thousand dead horses. One person claimed that twenty thousand people died each year from the maladies created by manure. The automobile was surely preferable to this.

The family car became a part of many positive feedback loops that created economic growth, drove things to extremes, and exposed society to vulnerabilities. Before the advent of the automobile, the trolley, and the railroad, cities were structured around the most prevalent form of interconnection—walking. Gross population densities were rarely less than thirty-five thousand residents per square mile. City neighborhoods were diverse, with few or none devoted exclusively to commercial, office, or residential functions. Work and living spaces were often integrated, with family members and apprentices living above or behind the shop or place of employment. During the Industrial Revolution, the slums built to house workers almost always surrounded the factories they served. Even as late as 1815, few people traveled more than a mile from where they lived to the place they worked.

In the middle of the nineteenth century, with the development of public transportation, the compact structure of the city began to change. Metropolitan Boston grew from a tightly packed merchant city of two hundred thousand residents in 1850 to an industrial metropolis. By 1900 there were more than a million residents within a radius of ten miles. Public transportation—the omnibus, a horse-drawn coach, later the horse-drawn trolley, and then the first electric trolleys—is what made that expansion possible.

These improved methods of transportation freed city dwellers from the unhealthy urban environment (including the pollution created by horses on the city streets), and enabled Americans to build homes in suburbs strung out along the railroad tracks. For the sake of convenience, these homes were almost always situated within walking distance of the trolley and railroad tracks, with new factories and places of work built along the tracks as well.

The physical connections of the day had constrained the population to space near the train tracks so people could commute to work, go shopping, and have access to entertainment.

With the automobile came an independent means of getting to and from wherever you wanted to go, and people no longer had to live near the tracks. Businesses had the freedom to locate wherever they chose and zoning laws allowed. As a result, in the aftermath of World War II, cities began to lose hold over their immediate environs. Suburbs that were once inextricably tied to the city via railroad and trolley lines were no longer just subsets of the urban world but self-supporting communities in a metropolitan region of which the city might have been a part, but not necessarily the only part. People no longer had to go to the city to shop, work, see a movie, visit a doctor, or eat at a restaurant, as these places and services were now available elsewhere. Populations spread across the rural landscape.

Today, the U.S.'s dependence on the automobile outstrips that of any other developed nation.

The story of the automobile is a perfect example of what I call the "vulnerability sequence." When dense interconnections create large amounts of positive feedback, the system can get driven to an extreme position, where lock-in occurs, and a vulnerability develops. The automobile's dependence on foreign oil—a vulnerability—is just one example of this phenomenon.

And how could Henry Ford possibly have foreseen such an outcome? It was Ford who, in the early twentieth century, envisioned a virtuous economic circle, a positive feedback process, which had at its center the Model T Ford, a low-priced automobile for the common man. Standardizing this one model over a number of years made it possible for Ford to develop specialized machinery for his assembly line and to produce parts at a significant saving in labor costs. Volume purchases of raw materials enabled the Ford Motor Company to negotiate low prices. As a consequence, Ford's vision was soon realized. Sales of the Model T Ford climbed from 10,660 cars in 1909 to 2,011,125 in 1923. As sales climbed, production costs declined, making it possible for more and more people to afford cars—including thousands of Ford's own workers.

Still, by 1922, only one person in ten owned a car, a fact that apparently did not go unnoticed by General Motors president Alfred P. Sloan, who believed that the more people who owned cars, the more others would want to as well. To accelerate this positive feedback process, Sloan developed a strategy that would first replace with buses the rail-bound trolleys on which people depended, then gradually wean bus riders off the buses and into cars. Putting this strategy into action, GM acquired the nation's largest bus manufacturer and operating company. Its initial foray into the bus business did not realize Sloan's vision, however. The buses were uncomfortable, smelled bad, and were frequently snarled in traffic. They did not, in any event, provide enough of an incentive to make trolley and train riders switch.

Nonetheless, convinced that Sloan's strategy was correct and that only its tactics were in error, GM, in partnership with Standard Oil of California, the Firestone Tire Company, and two other companies, formed the National City Lines to engage aggressively in a program of converting trolley lines into bus operations. By 1949, the company had been involved in the replacement of one hundred trolley systems in forty-five cities. At the time that National City Lines was organized, forty thousand trolleys were carrying riders. By 1965, only five thousand remained in service.

In order for the automobile to complete GM's triumph, however, America needed a better system of roads. Championing the cause, GM established the National Highway Users Conference to encourage state and local governments to use gasoline tax revenues exclusively for the construction of highways and roads. Also, succumbing in part to GM's heavy lobbying efforts, the federal government during the Eisenhower Administration became actively involved in expanding the interstate highway system. In 1955, Eisenhower argued for the system not only as a way to increase highway safety, cut the costs of car and truck operation, and reduce future traffic congestion, but also as a key component of national defense in case of nuclear attack.

The actions of GM and the government provided an important stimulus to the automotive industry. Better highways made it possible to commute over greater distances, encouraging people and places of employment to spread still farther across the landscape, thereby making it all the more difficult for public transportation to serve their needs. Cities that were designed prior to the automobile had shopping districts that lacked convenient parking. This inner-city paucity of parking locations led developers to build suburban shopping centers with large parking lots to accommodate customers' cars. The competition from these centers, in turn, weakened the cities' retail districts.

Everyone seemed a winner in the automobilification of America. High-wage jobs were created for union workers in the auto industry. Numerous corporations made money building cars and supplying parts and raw materials to the automotive industry. Shopping center developers loved the automobiles that carried customers to their malls. Home builders and the trade unions wanted to build new homes on vacant lands. Farmers loved the automobiles that made their farmlands close to the city more valuable. Millions found jobs servicing and repairing cars. Thousands of jobs were created building and maintaining roads and highways. Certainly there were few people in 1955 who would have wanted to shout down Charles E. Wilson, secretary of defense in the Eisenhower administration and former C.E.O. of General Motors, when he reportedly said, "What is good for General Motors is good for America."

As the American landscape evolved from one laid out in a linear fashion along rail and trolley lines to a multidimensional grid where people could live anywhere and commute to work anywhere, the viability of an effective public transportation system was undermined. By the mid-1950s, suburbs were sprawled across the countryside. At the same time, the automobile industry launched a vigorous campaign to get people out of trolleys and buses and into cars. Government support of the effort resulted in an unprecedented focus on the automobile.

Shortly thereafter, what with the changing of the landscape of the cities and the suburbs, the construction of highways and superhighways, and the difficulty of, and general lack of interest in, building economically viable transportation alternatives, the nation became dependent on the automobile, just as Pittsburgh had grown locked in on steel.

Not surprisingly, a number of vulnerabilities arose, including the environmental degradation of our air and water, traffic congestion, and urban sprawl. And most notable has become our dependence on foreign oil. In the 1950s, President Eisenhower expressed concern about what he considered heavy dependence on oil imports—some 20 percent of the nation's oil came from outside the U.S. Today, we import almost 60 percent, with unstable foreign governments a major source. Our extreme dependence on the gasoline-powered automobile—a form of lock-in—makes it virtually impossible for us to free ourselves from this vulnerability, at least not in the foreseeable future. In the nearly one hundred years since the first Model T rolled off the assembly line, we have traveled the road from early positive feedback to specialization in the automobile as a form of transportation and, ultimately, to lock-in, exposing us to vulnerabilities—all consequences, intended or otherwise, of living in an interconnected world.

FOURTEEN

Everything Is Interconnected—Part II

Frequently, we interconnect things to make them safer or because we hope to increase a system's efficiency. Creating interconnections is almost a knee-jerk response to the need to make systems safer. We tend to focus on the higher-probability events, paying less attention to the lower ones that could have catastrophic consequences. We just assume they will not happen on our watch.

The trouble with this approach is that it can lead to a system-wide catastrophe. In some cases, by reducing the chances that high-probability small problems will occur we increase the risk of lower-probability problems of catastrophic proportions—the Katrina effect.

When building power grids, we interconnect them so we can move power around the system to meet peaks in demand in disparate locations. Also, if a problem develops at one power station or a generator needs to be shut down for maintenance, other generating stations connected to the grid can be used to supply backup power to the system. This interconnectivity enables us to solve small problems and avoid many inconveniences. Of course, a failure in one part of the grid can cascade through the system and cause what might be called an electrical system contagion, resulting in lengthy blackouts that affect large swaths of the population.

The first serious indication of the North American power grid's vulnerability to major accidents came on December 9, 1965, when a line transporting power from Niagara Falls to New York City failed. Within minutes, thirty million people in the northeastern United States and in Canada were without electricity. Then, on July 13, 1977, the system failed again when lightning struck the Indian Point power plant in Westchester, New York, and nine million people lost their power. This time, however, in contrast to the outage of 1965, when New Yorkers helped one another through the crisis, trouble-makers took to the streets, setting fires, smashing store windows, and looting. In this case, the accident triggered a riot, a form of thought contagion.

On August 10, 1996, 7.5 million people in the western United States lost power when 175 generating units went out of service. Several days were required to restart the system, with the cost of the failure estimated at almost $2 billion. The West Coast was in the midst of an intense heat wave. Temperatures reached 106 degrees. The blackout took place on what happened to be the day of my younger daughter's wedding. We had rented a generator for a party tent (not because we anticipated a blackout but to power extra lighting for our guests), which made us self-sufficient. We were an island of light in a world of fast-approaching darkness, blissfully unaware of the problems facing 7.5 million of our West Coast neighbors. Being disconnected certainly has its advantages.

Once our happy guests left, they quickly learned about the problem. There were no stoplights working. People who needed gas were out of luck. The only lights in the hotels where they were staying were the emergency ones in the halls.

With these failures, the safeguards protecting the highly inter-connected systems were simply not up to what is arguably the most critical task of any power delivery system—maintaining power to customers. While in most cases the safeguards did protect the power grid itself from severe physical damage, they didn't protect those dependent on the system for comfort, livelihood, safety, and, in some cases, even their lives.

On April 8, 2009, *The Wall Street Journal* carried an article about how cyberspies had penetrated the computer systems used to control the power-generation networks. They had planted malicious code that could be turned on to disrupt the networks. National security officials suspected that this was the work of the Chinese or the Russians. The article stated, "The growing reliance of utilities on Internet-based communication has increased the vulnerability of control systems to spies and hackers, according to government reports."

Contagions that spread through power systems are another example supporting Charles Perrow's claims that you can make a complex system only so safe and that frequently the safety mechanism itself is involved in spreading the failure. So one of the first questions we have to ask when increasing the levels of interconnectivity in a system is: are we really making it safer or actually increasing the risk of a larger failure?

For instance, most experts would agree that, while some of the connections made in implementing a power grid do have demonstrable downsides, in general the benefits are greater than the problems they can cause. But there are many other important instances where such agreement does not exist.

Economists are fond of using the term "moral hazard" when talking about financial situations. A moral hazard occurs when financiers, investors, and individuals take big risks because they are secure in the belief that someone will bail them out if they fail. One of the reasons Treasury Secretary Henry Paulson did not bail out Lehman Brothers is that he felt it important to demonstrate to the financial community that the government would not save those companies that took undue risk. But financiers are not alone in succumbing to moral hazards. Companies underfund pension fund commitments, unions and government employees demand unrealistic levels of benefits, and recipients of Social Security and Medicare oppose reform because they are secure in the belief that someone will bail them out if the system is unable to pay them what they are owed.

In the case of pensions, we have opted in the past for defined-benefit systems that carry with them all the risks of the moral hazard. But in recent years companies have discovered that these plans are so risky that they are shedding them as rapidly as possible.* In 2005 an estimated 120 defined-benefit plans affecting 269,000 participants were terminated.

In these plans, both the companies and their employees make contributions, and the company guarantees that a retiree will receive a payment of a specified amount each month for the rest of his or her life. The beauty of this scheme from an employee's point of view is that he shares the risk with other employees and buys the equivalent of an insurance policy. His payments are guaranteed even if he lives fifty years after he retires and even if the pension fund makes poor investments and there isn't enough money in the plan to cover the payouts.

The guarantee by the company is a powerful form of interconnection. It connects the fate of the pension plan with the fate of the company.

To make things even better for the pensioner, companies are required to buy insurance from the Pension Benefit Guaranty Corporation (PBGC), a government entity that will guarantee payments in case the company fails. So with the company acting as the belt and the PBGC acting as the suspenders, anything going wrong is hard to imagine. Situations like this create ideal environments for moral hazards. Beneficiaries push for more benefits and lower contributions, secure in the knowledge that if they contribute too little the

---

*Speaking of moral hazards, many government agencies—local, state, and federal—still have such plans in place, on the assumption that if something goes awry and those plans become underfunded, the employees will pass the cost on to taxpayers.

company will pick up the bill and if the company fails the government (PBGC) will pay. Companies play along with the game as well. The payouts are future liabilities that future management will have to deal with. So if the current management underfunds the plans, corporate profits go up and the stock price rises, creating substantial wealth for a handful of executives.

The pension-guarantee system establishes yet another very powerful form of interconnection: it connects all of the defined-benefit plans. If too many of these fail, not enough money will remain in the pension-guarantee system to pay the retiree benefits. Also, failure of some plans can increase the insurance premiums that solvent plans have to pay. In principle, pension systems are a very simple construct. Employees and employers should pay enough into the system so that when that amount is augmented by the returns on the investments in the pension fund, the payments plus the returns will equal what the employees withdraw over the course of their retirements.

But nothing is that simple, of course, and much can go wrong. No one knows how long he or she will live. Suppose that as a result of a remarkable medical advance our life expectancies greatly increase. None of us can forecast investment returns accurately. Think of recent financial declines. No certainty exists that the investment manager in charge of the company portfolio will make the right decisions, not to mention the risk that forecasts we make today will not hold true many years into the future. For someone who goes to work at twenty-five, retires at sixty-five, and lives to eighty-five, forecasts must be reasonably accurate some sixty years into the future.

Defined-benefit plans have a simple solution for this problem. They connect a high-risk system to one with little perceived risk. For example, the employees at General Motors thought they were safe betting on the future of the biggest automotive manufacturer in the world. What they overlooked is that connections are a two-way street. Connecting a high-risk system to a low-risk one has the potential to bring down the low-risk system. But in the case of defined-benefit systems, the situation is even more dangerous. There is a connection few employees consider—the fact that their current income depends on the long-term viability of their employer. So if pension liabilities play a role in the failure of the company, employees not only see their pensions threatened but lose their jobs as well.

This phenomenon is not limited to corporations. For example, on May 23, 2008, the City of Vallejo, California, filed for Chapter 9 bankruptcy. Generous benefits and high salaries promised during the good times could not be supported by the tax base when things got rough. Many city employees lost their jobs as a result.

For the most part, government employees are covered by defined-benefit plans. Our Social Security system is a form of one. These plans are plagued by the same moral hazards that corporate plans face. Many are dramatically underfunded. For example, the Illinois State Employees' Retirement System has less than half the assets it needs to meet its commitments. The moral hazard in this case gets even worse than usual since the Illinois constitution guarantees that pensions will be paid before any other obligations.

The scenario for a typical troubled plan goes as follows: A company gets into trouble. It needs to borrow money. Lenders look at all of the company's liabilities. (United Airlines defaulted on a $9.8 billion pension liability.) The lenders see the mountain of liability on the books and decide not to lend to the company. The stock price drops, and the company can't raise money in the equity markets. Bankruptcy becomes the only option.

Their pension plans were not the only cause of the bankruptcy of United Airlines and Delta. But they played a role, as they have in the cases of many failed companies I've examined. The tight connection between the pension plans and other corporate assets and liabilities contributed to a positive feedback process that ultimately led to bankruptcy or corporate failure.

To be sure, the beneficiaries of these plans can always fall back on the Pension Benefit Guaranty Corporation. If their companies fail, their pension liabilities will be taken over by this federal agency, which limits the maximum payout to any individual to $54,000 per year. But even those receiving substantially less than that should not feel secure, because the PBGC is in a precarious financial condition. In 2005, the agency had a $22.8 billion unfunded liability.

In 2006, Congress passed the Pensions Protection Act, requiring companies to make added contributions to underfunded pensions. This was done in part to ensure that such plans wouldn't be dumped on the PBGC. While such a requirement might seem a logical solution, when it comes to complex systems, things are never as simple as they appear. Mercer LLC, a consulting company, estimated that some eight hundred companies it had examined began 2008 with about a $60 billion surplus in their pension funds, but by November 30, 2008, those companies had a total of $280 billion in unfunded liabilities. The stock market crash put even companies that were acting responsibly in tenuous positions. The law requires them to make billions in contributions just when money is difficult to borrow and cash is most needed, thus putting the companies' viability and their employees' jobs in jeopardy.

Students of accidents in tightly connected systems have argued that if there's a chance of seriously harmful failure, then the systems shouldn't be built in the first place. Currently there are an estimated forty-four million people covered by accident-prone defined-benefit plans. Overconnectivity has exacerbated the problem.

One of the riskiest benefit connections ever conceived is the one the government has chosen to make between Social Security and Medicare on the one hand and the federal budget on the other. The Congressional Budget Office had estimated that Social Security payouts would exceed payroll taxes in 2016, but that threshold was crossed in 2010—six years ahead of forecast. Medicare is currently estimated to have underfunded liabilities ranging from $30 to $90 trillion, depending on whom you believe.

Both of these programs will either have to be funded somehow or modified so that the government can meet its obligations. But there was no need to connect these programs to the federal budget when they were established. Both could have been set up as independent programs with no federal guarantees. Bureaucrats would then have been compelled to make tough decisions. Perhaps they would have been forced to raise tax revenues and premiums and to cut payouts and ration medical benefits sooner.

For years we benefited from the positive feedback loops that drove the automobile industry. The industry created jobs, not only for itself but also throughout the economy. The internal combustion engine made us the industrial powerhouse of the world. Unfortunately, those loops drove things too far.

My great concern is with interconnections like those involving the automobile, whose consequences we can't foresee. I am sure the members of the Soviet Politburo never foresaw the collapse of the Berlin Wall as a consequence of West German passports that connected East German citizens with the West, just as I'm certain that employees who pushed hard for management to guarantee their pensions never meant to bite the hand that was going to feed them.-

Most interconnections are benign, lulling us into complacency. The dangerous consequences of this complacency should teach us to be more alert, to be on the lookout for surprises, and to be more prepared before trouble strikes. One of the ideals of free trade is that it creates a growing world economy in which products are manufactured in optimum locations and made available to consumers at the lowest prices, so that everyone's standard of living goes up. But that ideal is fulfilled only if the global market grows quickly enough. Otherwise, the standard of living may rise in developing countries while it declines in developed countries. If developed countries want to profit from world trade, they need to keep their share of the world market from eroding too quickly. This becomes difficult to do if the Internet keeps facilitating offshoring across broad segments of the economy.

Levels of interconnectivity have always influenced the way markets operate. In the nineteenth century, the telegraph provided buyers with real-time knowledge of prices in distant markets, driving prices to converge over broad geographic areas. An efficient railroad system made it possible to move surplus goods to markets experiencing shortages. Distribution became more efficient, causing prices in different regions to converge.

Today, with fast, low-cost, and reliable transportation systems in place and up-to-the-minute global price quotes available via the Internet, regional markets have been transformed into a global one, with even the most perishable commodities available worldwide. Still, despite the enormous benefits for both producers and consumers, the enhanced interconnectivity has caused problems. Chief among these is the lack of "moral" and government control that can be exerted over market participants.

To understand how this problem has evolved, let's think about the market system that Adam Smith envisioned in the eighteenth century. According to Smith, individuals pursuing self-interests would create an automatically regulated market system that would serve the common good. Entrepreneurs driven by the desire to make a profit would build factories to make products to satisfy the needs of customers. Markets that produced large profit margins would attract competition, causing prices to fall and, as a result, demand to increase. In this manner, a market for a given product would be in a continual state of adjustment—a process that would ensure that consumers paid a fair price and that producers earned a reasonable profit.

But there was a catch. In what is known as the Tragic Vision of human nature (James Madison subscribed to it, as did Oliver Wendell Holmes Jr., Milton Friedman, and, of course, Smith himself), people are seen as inherently limited in knowledge, wisdom, and virtue. (As Immanuel Kant put it: "From the crooked timber of humanity no truly straight thing can be made.") In the Tragic Vision, our moral sentiments overlie a deeper foundation of selfishness, which isn't so much cruelty as a concern for our own well-being so integral to our makeup that we seldom reflect on it. As Smith argued in *The Theory of Moral Sentiments* (1759), "If [a man] were to lose his little finger tomorrow, he would not sleep to-night; but provided he never saw them, he would snore with the most profound security over the ruin of a hundred million of his brethren."

For the market system to function smoothly, Smith argued, participants had to be subject to certain controls: they had to "play fair," police their own actions, or depend on others in the community served by the market to police those actions for them. These controls would specifically include peers passing judgment on the immoral acts of participants, participants themselves feeling remorse and fearing punishment for doing something wrong, and a system of laws enforced by the government. If and when these controls were combined with the self-regulating market system Smith envisioned, not only would the needs of consumers and producers be met, but also the common good of society would be served. In this manner, man would be led as if by an "invisible hand" to promote ends that might not even be part of his original intention.

In today's highly efficient, tightly interconnected world markets, participants are frequently isolated from "the society" they serve. Concerned only with buying and selling, they barely consider possible damage to the community or any service to the common good. Nor is pressure to serve the common good exerted by the community at large. In other words, increased levels of interconnection have reduced moral control over markets, the ability of governments to regulate those markets, and the likelihood of rigorous self-regulation.

This is not to say that today's markets are totally unregulated. On the contrary, a system of laws enforced by governments does exist and does, to some extent, control and regulate much of what market participants can do. In the United States, for example, a long list of government institutions and mechanisms help regulate the behavior of market participants. Among these are, of course, Congress, the Federal Trade Commission, the Department of Justice Antitrust Division, the Securities and Exchange Commission, the U.S.

Food and Drug Administration, the Department of Transportation, various public utilities commissions, the Environmental Protection Agency, the Occupational Safety and Health Administration, and many others.

However, despite laws, regulations, and regulatory agencies—and just at a time when free market ideology is triumphing in many corners of the world—our interconnections are causing Smith's so-called invisible hand to lose its grip, as market participants increasingly pass the costs of their activities on to others without incurring any themselves.

This phenomenon is hardly new. What's new is the ease with which it occurs. For years, cigarette companies have been passing on the costs of treating the smoking-induced illnesses of their customers to society at large. Similarly, over decades factories and power plants in the Midwest have been externalizing the costs of acid rain caused by pollution onto citizens on the East Coast, where freshwater delivery systems have been compromised, forests have been blighted, and the fish in lakes and streams killed off. Had the cigarette companies or polluters been forced to pay for the damage they caused, they would likely have charged more for cigarettes or invested in effective pollution controls, so that the damage to society would have been diminished. Although recent court decisions, such as those against the cigarette makers, are forcing some market participants to internalize their costs, interconnections are making it increasingly difficult to pin down precisely what these costs are, where the damage is being felt, and under which nation's jurisdiction legal action should be taken, not to mention the difficulty of holding corporations to any standard of serving the common good.

Indeed, increased levels of interconnectivity have enabled companies to move wherever oversight is limited, tax rates low, and laws the least stringent, making it possible for corporations to become islands of enterprise free from moral constraints and legal controls.

As interconnection technologies have extended the reach of business and helped it migrate from physical to virtual space, the bonds between the pursuit of self-interest and the social control Smith envisioned have been further weakened. To see how this is happening, we need merely compare Smith's time to our own. In Smith's world, most people conducted business where they lived, and control, such as it was, rested with their neighbors—the same people they saw in church and who ran other local businesses. Smith argued that

> . . . in the race for wealth and honours and preferments . . . he may run as hard as he can, and strain every nerve and every muscle, in order to outstrip all his competitors. But if he should justle or throw down any of them, the indulgence of the spectators is entirely at an end. It is a violation of fair play, which they cannot admit of.

Corporations that now operate their businesses in third-world nations have an easier time than ever engaging in activities "they cannot admit of." While able to reduce their labor costs, avoid payment of taxes, and escape environmental and employee health and safety laws, these companies still enjoy the benefit of selling their products in their "home" markets, often to the same domestic workers they laid off, whose cost of support is being borne by the very society they abandoned. The most pressing question remains: what should we do to cope with the adverse effects of overconnectivity?

FIFTEEN

What Now?

G iven the dire perils of the overconnected world I've been anatomizing here, the questions now arise: What do we do about it? Do we learn to live with it, or do we set about dismantling it? Do we stringently regulate institutions that exploit overconnectivity to the detriment of society? Do we restructure governments in order to better deal with the challenges overconnectivity presents? Whether fortunately or not, our options are limited. We can't simply reverse history, and even if we could we wouldn't want to. We cannot retreat into a shell. We are too dependent on other places for things we don't make and resources we don't have. We need world markets for our products. And even if we tried to withdraw, we would still face overconnectivity challenges at home. Furthermore, our humanity and survival are inextricably linked to the fortunes of the world. Foreign ideas and beliefs will continue to influence our culture, just as our ideas, music, and entertainment influence nations abroad. The challenge then is not to hide but to confront overconnectivity head-on and deal with it.

Besides, the interconnected world we now live in offers too many benefits. Interconnections lie at the core of economic growth and development. They carried the freight in Silicon Valley. They built the framework supporting worldwide increases in productivity in manufacturing, transportation, service industries, and retailing.

Interconnections, especially those provided by the Internet, can offer us a transparent view of things, which helps us understand what is going right and what is going wrong. They shine a spotlight on unsavory behavior. Nongovernmental organizations empowered by the Internet can inexpensively get their message out and influence large groups. Financial information and SEC filings are instantly and easily available. Thousands of bloggers have become amateur investigative reporters. Most important, interconnections and, more specifically, the Internet, are the infrastructure supporting an unprecedented growth in knowledge—knowledge that could allow us to conquer disease, stop global warming, feed the world's population, and live more comfortable lives.

Each of us has already experienced the benefits of these new interconnections in some way or another, to some degree or another. It's easy to imagine a future that will extend these advantages. I live in a house in a rural part of the San Francisco Bay area that is tranquil and beautiful. If I want to experience the buzz of Silicon Valley, I need only get in my car and drive a few miles to my office, which is close to all the action. Yet increasingly I find myself working at home and commuting less. I do much of my shopping over the Internet these days, and more and more I seek my entertainment online. Just as the automobile once freed Americans from the constraints of the railroad, the Internet is liberating me from the strictures of suburban car traffic.

One can hypothesize about the future from these changes. Perhaps, in the Internet Age, the ideal location of our homes will change, and more people will want to live in remote places. As our homes become our work sites, they will need to contain more office space. Many of us who live more remotely will want home theaters. Who knows what the office buildings of the future will look like. Since the workers of the future will carry their files in their laptops or access them from a remote server, their offices will be portable. In more and more firms, people will share desks on a rotating basis.

Perhaps fewer office buildings will be needed. Imagine how the landscape will change as a result.

The automobile created the shopping mall, but as more of us shop in virtual stores there will be less need for malls and the retail outlets in them. Maybe malls and office buildings will be torn down and turned into apartment buildings. No one can predict these changes precisely, but history has shown that when big improvements are made in interconnection technology, the physical infrastructure of society is frequently transformed. The railroad transformed both Chicago and its environs. As ships were improved, the great seaports of the world were built to profit from them.

Still, as I've tried to make clear, the contemporary world's interconnections have spiraled so out of control and done so much damage that we need to do something to ameliorate that harm. If we can't sever the connections, we need at least to modify them somehow or turn down the amplification (or "gain," as engineers like to say), so that instead of an overconnected world we return to a highly connected one. But before arriving at any practical proposals, we have a very fundamental decision to make. Do we give priority to prevention or to opportunity? During the past centuries we have consistently tried to foster opportunity at the expense of prevention. I believe that the tide has now turned and we need to focus more attention on prevention. The challenge will be to avoid choking off progress in the process.

As I watched the 2008 financial crisis unfold, I kept thinking about the reactor meltdown at Three Mile Island some thirty years ago, the chaos in the control room as engineers struggled to find a solution, followed by the lucky guess made by the new shift supervisor to ignore procedures and override the system. Just as at Three Mile Island, during the 2008 financial crisis, multiple failures and events interacted—mortgage defaults, the collapse of the housing market, rising oil prices, the problems of Freddie Mac and Fannie Mae, defaults on credit card debt, rising unemployment, declining retail sales. Regulators and Treasury officials attempting to deal with the problem were watching the financial equivalent of the sixteen hundred control lights flashing in the nuclear reactor's control room while listening to the audible alarms from lobbyists, politicians, bankers, and the Big Three automakers. Officials were guessing at solutions, just as the new shift supervisor did, one minute injecting capital into the system, believing the problem was caused by a shortage of liquidity, and the next minute advocating the purchase of distressed assets from the banks to calm market fears about the uncertainty of the balance sheets of financial firms.

We know that Charles Perrow, the accident theorist, reached the conclusion that no complex, tightly connected system could ever be made 100 percent safe. He advocated never building such complex systems if they had the potential to do great harm when they failed. And he became a strong opponent of nuclear power plant construction. Unfortunately, humanity has no choice but to accept risk. In the case of nuclear power, civilization probably must either accept the risks of nuclear accidents or face the consequences of accelerated global warming. A tightly connected global financial system is another reality that we cannot will away. The system of global trade is still another. Notwithstanding periodic debates over privatization, the tight coupling of the Social Security and Medicare programs to the federal budget is yet another.

The principal difference between nuclear power plants and most of our other tightly connected systems is that the power plants have been designed from day one with the goal of avoiding accidents. Our other systems have been designed with less forethought and concern about problems that might develop. Too little effort has been given to making them safe. No one ever attempted to make the financial derivatives system as safe as a nuclear power plant.

In the past, that disregard might have been okay. Things happened more slowly. There was time to recover from mistakes. This is no longer the case, because things that used to take years or months now happen in days, hours, even minutes. We get to where we are going before we realize what is happening.

Of course, the danger in trying to make things as safe as reasonable is that we will bring financial systems, currency trading, and technological progress to a halt as we strive to build the ultrasafe system. We could reduce the number of freeway accidents by imposing a twenty-mile-per-hour speed limit. That action would be ridiculous because, although it would make the freeways safer, they would be nearly useless. The challenge will be to pick the right compromise between utility and safety.

Once we've come to understand the reality of overconnectivity, there are three things we must do to deal with it. First, we must reduce the levels of positive feedback, in order to minimize the accidents that such feedback engenders, the contagions it spreads, and its unintended consequences in general. Second, we must design systems so that they will be more robust and less prone to failure. Third, we must acknowledge the higher levels of connectivity that already exist and restructure our existing institutions to be more effective and adaptable.

The first step—dealing with positive feedback—takes us to the heart of the matter. Progress is driven by positive feedback, but so too are such malign developments as financial contagions, urban decay, dependence on the automobile, electronic viruses, e-mail spam, and many other economic and social blights. As Internet-driven connectivity continues to increase, so too does positive feedback. We are seeing its effects in online retailing, in book publishing, and in the newspaper industry. And it will certainly continue its unchecked course in the financial industry. We have already discussed numerous other areas that will feel its impact. As we learned from a variety of illustrations, when positive feedback runs rampant, it creates many unforeseen situations, some of which are beneficial but too many of which should be avoided at almost all cost.

One goal, then, is to introduce controls so we can throttle back and apply brakes that will keep things from racing out of control.

First, let's examine the regulation of banks and investment firms, the behavior of which, of course, lay at the heart of the recent meltdown. Regulation is one important way to reduce risk to depositors and—in the case of investment banks, which don't have depositors per se—to the economy as a whole. Both the Federal Reserve and the Treasury Department are considering new regulations for the industry with an eye toward turning down the gain. One of the best ways to do so would be to reduce the amount of leverage used by both financial institutions and individuals. This leverage reduction would prevent using very small amounts of money to buy and control large amounts of assets. For example, in 2007 investment banks were using $1 of capital to control $30 of assets, a leverage ratio of thirty to one.

Much of what we have seen recently is reminiscent of what happened after the 1929 stock market crash. Before the crash, an investor needed to put up just $1 to purchase $10 worth of stock on margin. In that case, the stock purchaser was leveraged ten to one. After the crash, regulators required that investors put up assets of at least $5 to buy $10 worth of stock on margin, effectively lowering the leverage ceiling from ten to one to two to one. This turned down the gain in the system since there wasn't as much money available to bid up the price of stocks.

Of course, the most profligate users of leverage in the more recent disaster were the major investment banks. Prior to the 2008 crisis, Morgan Stanley, Goldman Sachs, Bear Stearns, and Lehman Brothers were operating as shadow banks. Their regulator, the Securities and Exchange Commission, followed the Basel II rules (rules that aim to more closely link capital requirements to a bank's actual risk) that permitted them to leverage themselves thirty to one. Lehman Brothers was able to use just $22 billion in equity to support a balance sheet with $691 billion in assets. This meant that if the value of those assets declined by slightly more than 3 percent, Lehman would be bankrupt.

The shadow banks could not accept deposits, so they financed themselves in other ways. One of the most important was to use repurchase agreements, or "repos," which allow a borrower to use a financial security as collateral for a cash loan at a fixed rate of interest. Using these agreements, the shadow banks had access to large amounts of short-term money at favorable rates. Lehman alone obtained at least $182 billion through the use of repo agreements.

When investors grew nervous about the overleveraged Lehman, they refused to roll over the repurchase agreements. Lehman could not come up with the cash required, and the repo purchasers dumped the collateral on the market, driving down prices and adding power to the positive feedback processes that drove Lehman out of business. Six months prior to the demise of Lehman, Bear Stearns was sold to JPMorgan Chase for $10 per share, far below its fifty-two-week high of $133. Morgan Stanley and Goldman Sachs are now regulated banks and have greatly increased reserve requirements. This has helped reduce the gain in the system.

When investors lose confidence in an asset, they frequently run for the door, hoping to be the first to sell. As we know, such herd mentality drives prices lower. Forcing investors to think before they dump an asset can slow the decline. Commodity exchanges deal with this problem by establishing trading limits when prices fluctuate too much. For example, the Chicago Board of Trade limits the daily changes in price based on the prior day's trades. In the case of soybeans, the trading limit is 30 cents, which means that prices on a given day are limited to a range not 30 cents more or less than the price on the prior day. If that limit is reached, trading is halted. A simple halt to trading, one assumes, reduces the gain in the system by arresting thought contagions that lead to market volatility. Putting a stop to trading gives investors time to reflect instead of following the panicked herd.

Admittedly, good arguments for why investment firms should not be regulated more rigorously always abound. One of the strongest is that the freedom they are given to trade aggressively adds liquidity to the markets. That is certainly true. The more actively firms trade and the more securities they buy and sell, the more likely it is that sellers will be able to find buyers and thus convert their holdings into cash.

What is overlooked all too often is the fact that such aggressive trading, combined with significant leverage, can end up creating a shortage of cash when it is most needed. This happened in 2008. So we have to decide whether to restrict the markets so as to reduce the amount of liquidity available in normal times when its supply is adequate, in the hope of avoiding market meltdowns and the resulting lack of liquidity. In an overconnected world I would be in favor of such regulation.

Let me repeat that I am not arguing here for one particular set of approaches to solving the problem. I'm simply trying to make the case for a measure of caution that will effectively act as a throttle on the system.

Now let's examine taxation, another tool for reducing the gain in the system and, as a result, the amount of positive feedback. As an example of how it might have been used, think about the price of gasoline in the past. In the 1950s, had gasoline cost, say, $1 a gallon or more (which would have been the equivalent of about $3 today) instead of the 25 cents it did, society's physical infrastructure would probably look quite different today. There would be less urban sprawl, pollution, and traffic congestion. Mass transit might have emerged as the principal means of transportation. In any case, by taxing gasoline, the consequent higher prices would have weakened the positive feedback process that created an infrastructure defined by its dependence on the automobile.

Next, as another example of how taxation might be used as a control, consider currency trading, which has expanded considerably in recent years. Long ago, most cross-border currency transactions were made to support the trading of physical goods. As the world became more financially sophisticated, what started flowing between countries were transactions focused on *the value of the currency itself,* with no physical goods involved. In Iceland, for instance, speculators engaged in the so-called carry trade—borrowing money in countries with low interest rates and investing in the Icelandic krona, which then paid high interest rates. Today, we trade on the order of $3 trillion in currency per day, with speculative trading—that is, betting on fluctuations in exchange rates—estimated by currency traders to be as high as 90 percent. A lot of this currency is hot money flowing in and out of the economies of small countries at a moment's notice. (And if you predicted that I was going to point out that what facilitated the volume and speed of these transactions was none other than the Internet, you'd be absolutely right.)

The problem with these immense private cash flows is that they are often particularly large compared with the size of the local economies they flow in and out of and thus have the potential to overwhelm them. Economists have expressed concern over the attempts of small countries to put in place measures that would limit such cash flows, arguing that restrictions could do more harm than good. Yet such limitations would certainly turn down the gain in the system.

Some financial regulators have called for taxing financial transactions as a way of discouraging what they characterize as "socially useless" activities. A Tobin tax, named for Nobel laureate economist James Tobin, proposes to tax all spot conversions of one currency into another. The tax, intended to penalize short-term round-trip excursions into another currency, was suggested by Tobin in his Janeway lectures at Princeton in 1972, shortly after the Bretton Woods system of monetary management ended in 1971. Tobin suggested a rate of up to 1 percent, remarking that it would "throw some sand in the well-greased wheels" of speculative trading. Others have suggested rates as low as 0.1 percent percent, or 10 cents per hundred dollars. The higher the rate, the greater the reduction in gain. Of course, if the rate gets too high, world currency markets would come to a screeching halt.

Third, let's examine the device of pricing. By pricing, I mean putting a dollar amount on things we don't usually quantify or haven't quantified effectively enough. When things are properly priced, the amount of positive feedback in the system is greatly reduced.

For example, during the 2008 financial crisis, risk was underpriced. By this I mean simply that in the years leading up to 2008, people to whom it was risky to lend money were able to borrow at too low an interest rate, or too cheaply. In the case of bonds, leading up to the 2008 meltdown Standard & Poor's and Moody's were underpricing risk by giving triple A investment ratings to bonds that were being used to fund subprime (i.e., very risky) mortgages. Those ratings in turn fueled the positive feedback process inflating the bubble. The triple A ratings helped create an environment that provided cheap money to home buyers, drove up the price of homes, and encouraged owners to take on too much debt. In doing so, the triple A ratings encouraged irresponsible behavior that undermined the value of the securities the firms gave triple A ratings to. To sum up: in order to ensure that risk is properly priced, ways must be found to make the credit-rating services act more responsibly.

These agencies have traditionally been lightly regulated, or not regulated at all, in most countries, and in the United States they are, in addition, prone to conflicts of interest. Both the issuers of debt and the borrowers pay the agencies to rate the debt offerings. If a high credit rating is placed on the debt, money gets lent at lower interest rates. This is the financial equivalent of having the fox guard the henhouse. Alan Greenspan was sharply critical of the performance of the credit-rating agencies but believed the market would discipline them. That approach obviously did not work very well, and in the wake of the 2008 crisis several ways of regulating the rating agencies more effectively have been considered.

When the Internet interacts with financial processes, things happen quickly, and this means that any mispricing of assets can be exploited rapidly. If an asset is priced too high, speculators find ways to bet that the price will fall. If that asset happens to be a bond that a pension fund has counted on being very safe and conservative, billions can be lost overnight and retirement funds can vanish into thin air. When risk is underpriced, bonds become overpriced, making them big targets for speculators. The large losses that can occur make proper pricing of risk all the more important. The Internet amplifies mistakes.

Continuing our examination of pricing, let's look at what economists call externalities, or costs borne not by the parties involved in a transaction but by a third party somewhere down the line. In the case of e-mail, for instance, spammers pay only for the cost of sending the e-mail (which is often near zero) and not for the inconvenience caused to the recipients. Robert Morris paid nothing to send out the few dozen lines of computer code that composed his 1988 Internet worm, but it cost dozens of institutions tens of thousands of dollars to clear it out of their infected machines. Tobacco companies and smokers pass on to society the cost of smoking-related diseases. In recent years, cigarettes have been subjected to large "sin" taxes as a way to raise money to pay for these externalized costs.

In environments where lots of positive feedback is present, failure to put a price on externalities can lead to big problems. E-mail that is essentially free does not take into account the cost of all the externalities involved. And those costs have been very high. Because e-mail is so cheap, launching destructive computer viruses is very inexpensive. But dealing with these viruses costs companies and individuals billions of dollars a year. Similarly, free e-mail subsidizes junk e-mailers, who fill up in-boxes, making it harder to find important communications. Recipients of junk e-mail spend countless hours dealing with electronic trash. The cost to business of dealing with junk e-mail has been estimated to be as high as $10 billion per year.

Ideally, we would calculate the cost of the externalities and add them to the price of the product. However, decisions about an appropriate price are arbitrary, as no one really knows what the true costs are. In fact, overpricing externalities can be very damaging. That said, just because it is difficult to price things correctly doesn't mean the price should be set at zero.

Take gasoline, for example. I am convinced that CO_2 emissions have played an important role in climate change, but I have no idea what the charge should be for emitting, say, a ton of CO_2. In order to make an educated guess, we need to know how CO_2 emissions affect the rise in ocean levels and how much damage each inch of elevation costs. We also know that climate change affects rainfall—more rain in some regions and less in others. Should farmers in an area getting less rain be compensated, and, if so, how much? We also know that burning gas creates smog in many cities, and we know smog causes breathing difficulties for many people. How should that be priced? You see how gnarly this pricing can get.

In 2009, the right to emit a ton of CO_2 into the atmosphere was priced at around $18 in Europe, where firms buy carbon credits giving them the right to emit CO_2 at levels that exceed those permitted by the government. The 2009 price was relatively low because of the reduced generation of CO_2 during the economic slowdown. Several economists I have talked with think $30 a ton is a better number. I heard one environmentalist say that $135 was more appropriate. If you translate these prices into how much they would add to the cost of a gallon of gas, the result falls in the range of a dime to a dollar per gallon.

The only way I know to approach such a problem is to run experiments—start off charging a little and evaluate the effects. If small charges have no effect on CO_2 emissions, raise the price. If the price gets too high, causing great damage to the world economy, reduce it. This method of determining price amounts to having the price for CO_2 emissions set by the market, which probably does a better job than a government bureaucrat would.

When it comes to charging more for Internet use, junk e-mail would be a good place to start. We could start by setting a very low price and seeing how it works. If the results are favorable, then raise the price.

In the case of free trade, there too we have failed to price in externalities. When many companies export jobs, some are taking advantage of the fact that they do not have to meet tough environmental and product-safety standards, let alone just employment practices. As a result, the workers in developed countries end up paying the bill by losing their jobs.

As I pointed out earlier, the Internet and the positive feedback process have fueled the growth of free trade. Once again, things are being driven to extremes. In point of fact, neither developed nor developing countries benefit from things being driven to extremes. In developed countries middle-class workers have seen their standard of living decline. In developing countries, the migration to the cities has created pollution problems and poor working environments that threaten the health and safety of workers.

We can credit a phenomenon called information transparency for making us aware of many external costs in the first place. Thanks to the Internet, more information is available to greater numbers of people about everything from hazardous work environments to the role that deforestation plays in climate change. Transparency exposes problems such as unsafe working conditions and helps bring pressure to raise the costs of those causing the trouble.

But precisely how to raise those costs? Tariffs aren't necessarily the answer. However, I believe it is fair and reasonable to expect more from our trading partners when it comes to meeting some basic labor, environmental, and product-safety standards—equal, that is, to what we require of our domestic manufacturers. In the long run, meeting such demands would be in the interest of our trading partners as well. No country wants its image sullied by a reputation for unfair labor practices or for shipping unsafe toys and toothpaste around the world.

Such actions would slow down the growth in trade—not necessarily a good thing, of course, although it would also give countries time to adjust to the new realities of an overconnected world.

Thousands of realms are being driven to extremes by Internet-powered positive feedback processes—financial systems, free trade, e-mail, privacy, social networking, business monopolies, etc. I have made some suggestions about a few of them. We must learn to examine what is going on around us in a more critical fashion and attempt to understand the positive feedback processes at work. We must then make the critical decision as to whether we should throttle the processes back. In the past, we have usually argued that doing so would cause more harm than good. But after observing the current financial crisis, the meltdown in Iceland, and the loss of privacy, I have become convinced that we must now act more aggressively.

SIXTEEN

What Now, Continued: Katrina, Social Security, and a Tribe of Aborigines

My second suggestion for alleviating overconnectivity, as you'll recall, was to design systems differently from the outset, making them more robust and less prone to failure. This includes confronting problems early so they don't grow too large. For instance, when credit cards were first designed, the companies that issued them did not anticipate the levels of fraud and identity theft we see today. As a result, systems were designed with inadequate security, in part because security measures would have made the cards more difficult to use and thus slowed down market acceptance. Today hundreds of thousands of card numbers can be stolen from a single Web site, then sold over the Internet for a few dollars each. In hindsight, that design decision seems downright irresponsible.

The first principle in designing systems differently is to anticipate the effects of overconnectivity. This is far easier said than done, as overconnectivity creates very complex systems whose performances are extremely unpredictable. Still, there are a few things we can do. One is to avoid deluding ourselves into thinking a mere patch will forestall disaster. Second, we can adopt a conservative approach and design systems with greater safety margins. Third, we can avoid creating unnecessary interconnections. And last but by no means least, we should avoid building systems that are inherently dangerous in the

first place. This is what Perrow meant when he argued against building nuclear power plants.

There's a lot to be learned from a hurricane. As I've said, the
devastating effects of Katrina showed us the perils of putting Band-
Aids on problems (like building inadequate levees to prevent relatively minor flooding), then ignoring them so as to invite still larger
catastrophes in the future. The subprime crisis is the most recent
example of the Katrina effect. For a long time, government officials
and regulators had been agonizing over potential problems at Fannie
Mae and Freddie Mac. In 2001, the Bush administration made
attempts to reform these corporations but failed in Congress. As late
as 2006, John McCain and nineteen other senators sent a letter to the
Banking, Housing, and Urban Affairs Committee of the Senate urging it to consider regulatory reform of Freddie Mac and Fannie Mae.
Their effort died in committee. Congress's actions were similar to
those of the Orleans Levee Board, which had numerous opportunities
to strengthen the levees years before Katrina hit but chose instead to
ignore the problem.

When it comes to both Social Security and Medicare, we are using
Band-Aids to deal with their problems, making a Katrina-like crisis
imminent. As will be mentioned further on, both of those systems
could have been designed in ways that would have greatly reduced the
probability of disaster.

As a next step, we ought to think about approaching financial
risk more conservatively, in order to avoid many of the problems we
encountered in the current subprime crisis. During the Depression,
great pressure was brought to make more affordable home loans
available. In 1938, Franklin Roosevelt led the creation of the Federal
National Mortgage Association—Fannie Mae—in an effort to
increase home ownership and make housing more affordable. The
mortgage business was begun in the 1930s in response to a liquidity
crisis during the Depression. Back then, a 20 percent down payment
was considered the minimum amount a bank would approve. In 1934,

Morton Bodfish, the head of a Congressional committee overseeing the mortgage industry, said that lending *as much as* 80 percent of a house's appraised value was a risk worth taking only when a personal relationship existed between the lender and the borrower. "We can go that high," Bodfish said, "when we know a man, and know him well."

Over time, those standards were reduced, and the world became overconnected. In such an environment, you are asking for trouble when you engage in irresponsible lending practices. During the height of the subprime bubble, people were able to buy homes with no money down at all and no documentation to support their reported income. In 2006, 61 percent of home buyers receiving subprime loans had credit scores so low they couldn't qualify for *less* costly conventional loans. Between 2000 and 2007, the dollar value of the subprime loans increased by $2.5 trillion.

The environment did just what one would expect it to have done: it pushed things to excess, then punished us for giving in. In the long run, the liberal loan policies damaged the very people they were intended to help, and those borrowers became the ones hardest hit by the ensuing crisis.

Conservative approaches require us to build greater safety margins into our systems. When the Great Depression was still fairly fresh in our collective memory, we used to do just that. As individuals, we saved money. We paid off our mortgages and planned to retire without having to make home payments. Many of us sold off our expensive urban dwellings to the next generation and retired to lower-cost retirement communities in Florida or Arizona. There was a time, during the 1970s, when the national debt was less than 40 percent of our gross domestic product. In 2008 it was around 70 percent and rose to about 85 percent by the end of 2009.

A nation of responsible savers, not wanton consumers, comprises a society with safety margins, one in which businesses are encouraged to operate with strong balance sheets and not leverage themselves beyond all reason. This caution is especially important when the business environment is driven by the Internet. In periods of rapid change, businesses frequently have to restructure to survive. To do so takes both cash and time. Highly leveraged companies frequently lack the assets to restructure. Newspapers are a perfect example. They have been in decline for years, losing subscribers and advertisers while still generating cash. This has made it possible for them to take on huge amounts of debt—which is precisely what Sam Zell did when he purchased the Tribune Company.

The Tribune Company owned a number of trophy properties, such as the *Chicago Tribune,* the *Los Angeles Times,* television stations, prime office buildings, and the Chicago Cubs baseball franchise. In 2007, Zell put up $315 million of his own money, then borrowed $8 billion more to complete the purchase and take the company private—a leverage ratio of twenty-six to one. By the time he was through, the Tribune Company was saddled with $13 billion in debt. Under the strain, the company was forced to declare bankruptcy in 2008.

Many other companies have undergone leveraged buyouts in recent times and run into similar problems. On March 23, 2009, alone, the following companies filed for bankruptcy: Indalex Holdings (an aluminum manufacturer), Sportsman's Warehouse, Morton Industrial Group (the parent of a supplier to Caterpillar), and Bi-Lo LLC (a supermarket chain). This number of bankruptcies was the most that Jennifer Rossa, a reporter for *The Wall Street Journal,* could recall happening on a single day. There are always specific reasons in any bankruptcy. Unfortunately, in stressful times, companies need some cushion to be able to recover from operating problems and mistakes. When burdened with debt, they have to execute perfectly or they will fail.

If governments are going to create some slack in the system in order to maneuver, they will have to find ways to live within their means. States should have surpluses in general funds. As for the federal government, it should find ways to reduce its debt. Think how much better off we would have been in coping with the financial crises that swept the globe in 2008 if consumers had been less burdened with debt, if businesses had been less leveraged, and if the government had been operating with a surplus or modest deficit. If you are stretched to the limit, when a big problem occurs your options are far fewer. And in overconnected environments, the chances of a big problem happening are much higher, so every individual and institution needs more reserves. The challenge then for government is to encourage more responsible behavior and lead by example. We've done just the opposite, of course.

Policy makers should be constantly vigilant about interconnections and their potential consequences. There are many cases in which interconnections can be broken—well before they become dangerous—with relatively minor repercussions. Breaking those connections later, once they have gathered momentum, becomes almost impossible. Imagine what it would take, for instance, to dismantle the huge databases about our lives that commercial companies have amassed. The creation of these large databases of information about consumers might be part of the natural course of capitalism, but in this case consumers are not likely to benefit much from the information products created by ChoicePoint or InfoUSA. The data these information-aggregation companies collect are used mainly for marketing credit cards and selling vacations, automobiles, and various other consumer products, as well as targeting donors to philanthropic and political causes. But keeping all these data in a single location can result in the possibility of identity theft and consumer fraud and may create an accident-prone environment in which files get lost and stolen. If the government had prohibited these connections from being made in the first place, we would be facing far fewer threats to our individual privacy.

One of the reasons I wrote this book was to sensitize people to the potential perils of interconnections. I have focused primarily on the Internet, but I hope I've also made it clear that other types of interconnections also present us with challenges. No need existed to build certain interconnections into some of our most important federal programs. Take Social Security and Medicare, for example, whose benefits are paid out of the federal budget. Today Social Security represents a little less than 5 percent of the gross domestic product. It is forecast to grow to over 6 percent by 2040. However, as soon as 2017, the administration is predicted to be paying out more in benefits than it is taking in. A similar problem exists with Medicare, which currently represents about 5 percent of the gross domestic product and is expected to rise to over 10 percent by 2040. The difficulty with all of this is that current federal tax revenues run about 18 percent of the GDP. So by 2050, to judge from projected increases, Social Security and Medicare will be consuming 90 percent of the federal budget—an impossible situation.

Over the years, a number of solutions to the looming Social Security problem have been proposed: raise the retirement age; change the way the increase in payouts is indexed to inflation; reduce the payouts to wealthy individuals.

Social Security could have been established from day one as an independent mandatory federal retirement savings program with separate assets used exclusively to pay retirement benefits. If the assets weren't there, the program would be unable to write the checks. This would have forced the government to act more responsibly sooner.

Separating Social Security from the federal budget would have accomplished two things—deprived the latter of money it should not have been spending and forced it to act more conservatively as a result. Everyone knows we don't have to face the Social Security issue now, since federal funds can be used to bail out the system when the crisis hits later—a colossal moral hazard. The same goes for Medicare. But now we are really faced with a challenge. The government may have taken on so much debt to deal with the 2008 financial crisis that it may not be in a position to bail out Social Security.

As we turn to our next meliorative proposal—to avoid the creation of dangerous systems from the start—we can take another lesson from the 2008 financial crisis. In its wake, several institutions that had grown too big to fail had been exposed. Among them were Fannie Mae, Freddie Mac, and AIG, the American International Group insurance company. The government bailed out the ten largest banks because it was concerned about the potential impact of their failures on the economy. That is, those institutions were so tightly connected to so many others that if any single one were to fail the result might bring down significant portions of the system. And Iceland offers the example of a country that created institutions too big to fail in a country too small to save them.

In early 2010, Treasury Secretary Timothy Geithner proposed a way to defray the cost of bailing out the U.S. financial industry: slap a tax on financial institutions with assets of more than $50 billion. "We're doing it in a way that effectively puts a tax on leverage," he said in an interview, adding that the specter of a tax could help curb some of the risky practices that caused the crisis.

Paradoxically, in highly connected environments, one of the key strategies for corporate survival is to become big. A service company needs to achieve massive scale to serve the accounting and legal needs of its customers. And large manufacturing companies demand large, robust suppliers. Global companies want to deal with law and accounting firms that can provide them with support no matter where they are operating. The need for such size is one reason why just a handful of global accounting firms exist. The same situation is evolving in the legal profession. We have created monstrous banks, each with more than a trillion dollars in assets, to meet the financing needs of companies operating around the globe. And to be a successful automotive manufacturer, you must be very big to achieve economies of scale.

One thing I learned in my career at Intel was that to serve the needs of large customers, you have to be pretty big yourself. Large automotive customers, such as Ford, were not interested in dealing with small semiconductor manufacturers. At the time Intel started doing business with Ford, in the late 1980s, although we had revenue in the hundreds of millions, we were almost too small for its consideration. The changing perspective of entities such as Ford was just the start of a trend on the part of large companies looking to narrow their supplier base. In 2009, Sony announced that to save costs it would cut the number of parts suppliers in half. General Motors has aggressively reduced the number of its suppliers. Other companies are doing the same.

In environments with lots of positive feedback, companies can remain small and profitable only if they are willing to serve niche markets with specialized needs. The more positive feedback, the more likely we are to see institutions that are too large to fail—Fannie Mae, Freddie Mac, Citigroup, AIG, and General Motors.

This trend can be dealt with in a number of ways. One is not to allow institutions to grow too large. Another is to regulate institutions that are already too big to fail so as to reduce the likelihood of failure. In the case of financial institutions, regulation is undeniably the right approach. That is precisely what regulators in Europe and the United States are now attempting to do.

With other businesses the solution is less obvious. In an overconnected world, many markets will allow only gigantic companies to survive. You can't be a small automotive manufacturer and participate in the broad market. The government of Japan is stuck with Toyota, which is just beginning to show the vulnerabilities that large size creates. Unfortunately, the best solution may be to let "can't fail" corporations fail anyway.

Saving these corporations is extremely difficult. After a bailout, they are usually so enfeebled and dysfunctional that they have trouble succeeding. And once bailed out they frequently fail again. Chrysler was saved from bankruptcy in 1980 with a $1.2 billion government bailout and then failed again in 2009, eventually to be purchased by Fiat. Although the effects of such failure can be very traumatic, it would probably not bring down the rest of the economy with it. Often a buyer will swoop in and pick off the valuable pieces, as Fiat did with Chrysler. In the long run, such a course will probably turn out to be less traumatic and certainly less expensive. On the other hand, when in late 2008 the government decided to save General Motors, the financial environment was so fragile that GM's failure could have driven the U.S. economy into a much deeper recession. Saving GM was probably the right thing to do during that treacherous time.

A third way to deal with overconnectivity is to acknowledge the higher levels that already exist and restructure our institutions so they can operate effectively in the new environment. Many institutions have simply not adapted to the new world of the Internet. Those that can need to do so with adjustments ranging from slight alterations to complete restructuring. Those that can't should be eliminated. No good will come of making minor changes and hoping for the best.

Adjusting to the new environment will require thought and action different from what we have done in the past. Policy makers used to try modifying slapdash solutions as they muddled along. In fact, in his classic 1959 article on social policy, "The Science of Muddling Through," Charles Lindblom argued that such an approach was ideal—to make incremental changes and modifications based on the insights and understandings gleaned from the process of implementation. But this won't work in today's overconnected environments. Tinkering with existing dysfunctional systems will probably never create ones that function well.

Let's take two obvious examples from the financial world. We badly need to improve our regulatory systems, because they have not kept up with the increased levels of connectivity. Such Internet-enhanced innovations as packaging and marketing subprime mortgages, creating new derivative products, or devising high-frequency trading schemes have clearly outrun the regulators.

Two different approaches have been proposed for reshaping the regulatory environment. One, suggested by Christopher Cox, the former chairman of the SEC, would combine that commission and the Commodity Futures Trading Commission (CFTC) into a single body.

But Walter Lukken, at the time of Cox's proposal the top official of the CFTC, responded that such an organization would be "ineffective and would only reinforce our outdated regulatory structure." Lukken proposed switching from the current inadequate regulatory approach to a "principles-based" system, or one in which regulators articulate goals or principles (such as disclosing material information to investors) without spelling out each and every disclosure that must be made. The justification for this would be the impossibility of spelling out regulations in a timely fashion.

Stephen Schwarzman, the CEO of the Blackstone Group, a large financial firm, has pointed to the need for a common set of cross-border accounting principles. His proposal includes replacing the hodgepodge of domestic regulatory agencies with regulatory bodies that oversee all institutions participating in markets, regardless of charter, location, or legal status.

The power of governments has historically been limited by the geography they control, yet with no small measure of help from the Internet the problems they are dealing with have grown with little regard for geographic boundaries. Just think again about Iceland.

Christopher Cox's incremental approach would not only protect outdated bureaucracies but also borrow a page from Lindblom's theory of muddling through. It's doubtful that it would ever lead to the revolutionary changes proposed by Lukken and Schwarzman, who recognize the effects of overconnectivity.

At the heart of the Lukken-Schwarzman argument for the wholesale replacement of existing regulatory bodies is the realization that minor fixes of existing organizations simply won't solve the problem. This is yet another example of new levels of interconnectivity requiring new types of organizational structures. But Schwarzman goes even further, implying the need for a powerful transnational regulatory agency.

In the future we will increasingly face situations where tinkering with existing institutions won't solve problems that, because of new interconnected environments, will demand more drastic and timely approaches.

Fifty years ago, my mother, who served on the national board of Girl Scouts of America, attended an executive meeting in Atlanta. At one point during a discussion about some of the problems facing the organization in the latter part of the twentieth century, one of the fine Southern ladies at the meeting commented, "Wasn't the world wonderful before progress?"

I loved that remark and have always wondered how the woman who made it would have enjoyed living in a cave. But now I find myself growing more sympathetic to her position. Progress is wonderful, but only as long as society can keep up with it.

One of my hopes in writing this book is that by thinking more deeply about the implications of the Internet, people will be better equipped to manage their lives and institutions. Knowing how hard it will be for us in the United States to confront these challenges, I can only imagine how difficult this will be for less developed countries. And I worry about the social and spiritual upheavals that may accompany these changes.

History is filled with examples that support this point. One is the Yir Yoront, an aboriginal tribe that lived for more than fifty thousand years at the mouth of the Coleman River on the Cape York Peninsula in Northern Australia. An early Stone Age tribe, its culture was based on a totemic system laden with myth that effectively reinforced the status quo and resisted change. For example, although the Yir Yoront knew about canoes from observing a neighboring tribe, they allowed no place for them in their own totemic system. So the tribe continued to ford a crocodile-infested river by holding on to logs.

Playing a significant role in their social structure was the polished stone axe. Crafted from scarce stones, these axes were rare and highly coveted, conferring great stature upon their possessors. Only the tribe's male elders were allowed these axes, which made the tools a powerful symbol of masculinity. Stone axes also played a role in the trading relationships between the Yir Yoront and other groups, and they were an important element in the tribe's rites and rituals.

In the latter part of the nineteenth century, missionaries bent on civilizing the isolated tribe brought with them metal tools, among them short-handled steel axes. Believing that these would make the Yir Yoront more productive, the missionaries presented them not only to the tribe's older men but also to its young ones, and to women as well. Even children were given steel axes.

As a result of this well-intentioned act, the Yir Yoront's social order, over the next few decades, suffered a complete collapse. With the symbols of power diminished by the proliferation of steel axes, tribal leaders lost their authority. Subordinates became independent agents. Trading relationships broke down. Participation in annual ceremonies declined; celebrations lost their joy. Indeed, the ready availability of steel axes served to undermine the Yir Yoront's entire totemic system, which had given meaning to life and formed the very basis of their society.

Although it is dangerous to draw too many conclusions about the potential fate of contemporary society from this one example, the Yir Yoront illustrate the damage that interconnection—in this case, the tribe's contact with the outside world—can do to an underconnected culture, particularly one steeped in the status quo and resistant to change. I believe the steel axe is also an apt metaphor for the power— and occasional ferocity—of the change the Internet can bring in its wake. The Internet, and the role it played in the subprime crisis, is a modern-day version of the steel axes given the Yir Yoront. As we struggle with the erosion of an ownership society that so aggressively encouraged the purchase of homes and the consequent economic turmoil, we are experiencing some of the same "cultural disintegration, and a demoralization of the individual" that the Yir Yoront did with the loss of their Stone Age axes.

Just as the steel axe should have improved the lives of the Yir Yoront, the Internet should make our existences better. But the

Internet will achieve this only if we learn how to accommodate it. At times I have wondered if my technologist friends and I weren't every bit as naïve as the missionaries. We brought the world the tools and believed society could only benefit. None of us would have predicted the extent to which our social and economic structures would be transformed. Now we find ourselves at the peak of the evolutionary pyramid, facing what H. G. Wells called the "inexorable imperative" to adapt or perish. Wells was referring to the natural world, but in the twenty-first century we have no choice but to adapt to an environment transformed by our own inventions. This new environment is filled with opportunity, but whether we seize it or let it hold us hostage is our decision to make.

Notes

I began working on this book in 2000. By that time it was clear that the Internet had changed the world. Many insightful books had either alluded to or had been written about its effects—Frances Cairncross's *The Death of Distance*, Thomas L. Friedman's *The World Is Flat*, Manuel Castell's *Information Age Trilogy*, etc. Many of the writings about networks and complex systems provided insights into what was happening. But none of them provided me with a truly deep understanding of what fundamental force was behind Internet-driven change.

At the same time, I became increasingly uncomfortable with all the idealized models economists were using to forecast the future. How could anyone believe he or she could accurately model an extremely complex nonlinear system?

At that point I turned to history and began studying other great technological changes in hopes of finding some answers. In my travels into the past, I stumbled upon papers by Eugene Wigner and W. Ross Ashby. Wigner had proved that under certain conditions any large interconnected environment ended up with positive eigenvalues. Ashby had observed that as their complexity increased, many systems reached a critical point where they became unstable. At that point a light went on in my head. I theorized that increasing and strengthening interconnections would create large amounts of positive feedback in a system, creating rapid change, driving situations to extremes, making the system accident-prone, and supporting contagions.

The bursting of the Internet bubble in 2000 was the first evidence of this phenomenon. The Internet created the stocks inflating the bubble; it transmitted the rumors that drove up the prices of the stocks; it supported the thought contagion that accompanies all economic bubbles; it made day trading possible by enabling individuals to make low-cost trades from their desks at work and in their living rooms at home. But those examples alone could not support a broader argument. That is where my search through history came in.

John Padgett at the Santa Fe Institute suggested that I might find some answers in the history of cities. John Staudenmaier suggested I look at William Cronon's book *Nature's Metropolis: Chicago and the Great West*. Much of the material in the first chapter is based on what I discovered in those readings. What surprised me most was that an improvement in a physical interconnection, namely the railroad, was having effects so similar to those caused by the Internet—among them, new financial products, such as derivatives, virtual enterprises, etc. When I read Gary Fields's book *Territories and Profits*, I was struck by how the railroad was creating virtual enterprises and how Swift had used it to disintermediate East Coast butchers. His story about Swift was shockingly similar to ones being written about travel agents today.

Thomas J. Misa, director of the Charles Babbage Institute for the History of Information Technology at the University of Minnesota and the author of *A Nation of Steel: The Making of Modern America, 1865–1925*, helped fine tune the section on Andrew Carnegie.

Charles Perrow's book *Normal Accidents: Living with High-Risk Technologies* and his discussion of Three Mile Island that I have referred to in this book and his stories about collisions of ships at sea convinced me that financial systems that increasingly depended on the Internet and massive databases of personal information were going to prove to be extremely accident-prone environments, and many of them should never have been built.

Brian Fagan's book *The Long Summer* begins with catastrophes faced by New Orleans as the levees kept failing. When placed in the context of other vulnerability sequences I had learned about, the Katrina Effect came into focus. I am also indebted to Constantine Magin, who did the research on the 1987 market crash, which to my knowledge was the first financial contagion in which machines did much of the thinking for people and drove prices down.

When Iceland became a victim of speculation, I surmised that the Internet must have played a role. How else could a tiny country in the middle of the Atlantic become a big financial player in world markets? I sought out someone who could help me find the answer and made a virtual acquaintance with Alda Sigmundsdóttir ("daughter of Sigmundur"). Alda did much of the research for the chapters on Iceland. When I learned about the movement of money to and from Iceland, I became interested in bills of exchange. Jean Andreau's story about Cicero provided an intriguing frame of reference.

When the history of financial manias and panics caught my attention, one of the first books I read was Charles Mackay's classic work, *Extraordinary Popular Delusions and the Madness of Crowds*. I have cited many of his stories. They provide great insights into the workings of positive feedback, many supported by that very traditional interconnection technology—rumors.

Much of the material about the 1929 market collapse is based on John Kenneth Galbraith's book *The Great Crash—1929*. For help in understanding Adam Smith's views on human nature, I relied on Steven Pinker's excellent book *The Blank Slate: The Modern Denial of Human Nature*. I used Robert O'Harrow's excellent book, *No Place to Hide,* as a source for much of the information on ChoicePoint. I have relied on Gale Stokes's book *The Walls Came Tumbling Down* for much of the material on the collapse of the Soviet Union. J. Stephen Lansing's *Priests and Programmers* was the source of the material on the Green Revolution in Bali.

Bibliography

Adams, Henry. *The Education of Henry Adams,* Chapter 34. www.bartleby.com/159/34.html

Adams, James. *The Next World War.* New York: Simon and Schuster, 1998.

Ambrose, Stephen E. *Nothing Like It In The World.* New York: Simon and Schuster, 2000.

Anderson, Christopher. "A Survey of The Internet: The accidental superhighway." *The Economist,* 1 July 1995.

Anderson, Philip W.; Arrow, Kenneth J.; and Pines, David. *The Economy as an Evolving Complex System.* A Proceedings Volume in the Santa Fe Institute Studies in the Sciences of Complexity. Reading, MA: Perseus Books, 1988.

Andreau, Jean. *Banking and Business in the Roman World.* Cambridge: Cambridge University Press, 1999.

Andrews, Anthony P. *First Cities.* Washington, D.C.: Smithsonian Books, 1994.

Arrighi, Giovanni, and Silver, Beverly J. *Chaos and Governance in the Modern World System.* Minneapolis: University of Minnesota Press, 1999.

Arthur, W. Brian; Durlauf, Steven N.; and Lane, David A. *The Economy as an Evolving Complex System, II.* A Proceedings Volume in the Santa Fe Institute Studies in the Sciences of Complexity. Reading, MA: Perseus Books, 1997.

——. *Increasing Returns and Path Dependency in the Economy.* Ann Arbor, MI: University of Michigan Press, 1998.

——. "Positive Feedbacks in the Economy." Scientific American, 262, 92–99, Feb. 1990

Axelrod, Robert, and Cohen, Michael D. *Harnessing Complexity.* New York: Basic Books, 2000.

Bairoch, Paul. *Cities and Economic Development.* Chicago: University of Chicago Press, 1988.

Barabasi, Albert-Laszlo. *Linked.* New York: Plume, 2003.

Barnet, Richard J., and Cavanaugh, John. *Global Dreams.* New York: Simon and Schuster, 1994.

Barnett, Thomas P. M. *The Pentagon's New Map*. New York: G. P. Putnam's Sons, 2004.

Barry, John M. *The Great Influenza*. New York: Viking, 2004.

Berkowitz, Edward D., and McQuaid, Kim. *Creating the Welfare State*. Lawrence, KS: University of Kansas Press, 1992.

Berners-Lee, Tim, with Mark Fischetti. *Weaving the Web*. New York: HarperCollins Publishers, 1999.

Blackmore, Susan. *The Meme Machine*. Oxford: Oxford University Press, 1999.

Boyle, James. *Shamans, Software, and Spleens*. Cambridge, MA: Harvard University Press, 1996.

Braudel, Fernand. *Capitalism and Material Life 1400–1800*. New York: Harper & Row, 1967.

——. *The Perspective of the World*. Berkeley: University of California Press, 1992.

——. *The Structures of Everyday Life*. Berkeley: University of California Press, 1992.

——. *The Wheels of Commerce*. Berkeley: University of California Press, 1992.

Brook, James, and Boal, Iain A. *Resisting the Virtual Life*. San Francisco: City Lights, 1995.

Bruner, Robert F., and Bernstein, William J. *The Panic of 1907*. Hoboken, NJ: John Wiley & Sons, 2007.

Buchanan, Mark. *Nexus—Small Worlds and the Groundbreaking Science of Networks*. New York: W.W. Norton, 2002.

Burke, James, and Ornstein, Robert. *The Axe Maker's Gift*. New York: G.P. Putnam's Son's, 1995.

Burstein, Daniel, and Kline, David. *Road Warriors*. New York: Penguin, 1995.

Cabadas, Joseph. *River Rouge: Ford's Industrial Colossus*. St. Paul, MN: MotorBooks/ MBI Publishing Company, 2004.

Caballero, Ricardo J. *Macroeconomic Volatility in Reformed Latin America*. Washington, D.C.: Inter-American Development Bank, 2001.

Carlson, Richard, and Goldman, Bruce. *2020 Visions*. Stanford, CA: The Portable Stanford Book Series, 1991.

Cairncross, Frances. *The Death of Distance*. Cambridge, MA: Harvard Business School Press, 1997.

Carr, Nicholas. *The Big Switch*. New York: W.W. Norton, 2008.

Chandler, Alfred D., Jr. *The Visible Hand*. Cambridge, MA: Harvard University Press/Belknap Press, 1977.

Claessens, Stijn, and Forbes, Kristin J. *International Financial Contagion*. Boston: Kluwer Academic Publishers, 2001.

Coase, R. H. *The Firm, the Market, and the Law*. Chicago: University of Chicago Press, 1990.

Corsetti, Giancarlo; Pesenti, Paolo; and Roubini, Nouriel. *What Caused the Asian Currency and Financial Crisis, Part II: The policy debate*. National Bureau of Economic Research, September 1998.

Cronon, William. *Nature's Metropolis: Chicago and the Great West*. New York: W.W. Norton, 1991.

Crosby, Alfred W. *The Measure of Reality*. Cambridge: Cambridge University Press, 1997.

Davidow, William H., and Malone, Michael S. *The Virtual Corporation*. New York: Harper Business Collins, 1992.

Davies, Glyn. *A History of Money*. Cardiff: University of Wales Press, 1994.

Davis, Mike. *The Monster at Our Door*. London: The New Press, 2005.

Dawkins, Richard. *The Selfish Gene*. Oxford: Oxford University Press, 1989.

De Landa, Manuel. *A Thousand Years of Nonlinear History*. New York: Zone Books, 1997.

de Sola Pool, Ithiel. *Technologies of Freedom*. Cambridge, MA: Harvard University Press/Belknap Press, 1983.

Diamond, Jared. *Collapse*. New York: Viking, 2005.

——. *Guns, Germs, and Steel*. New York: W.W. Norton, 1997.

Dinkelspiel, Frances. *Towers of Gold*. New York: St. Martin's Press, 2008.

Dorn, James A. *The Future of Money in the Information Age*. Washington, D.C.: Cato Institute, 1997.

Dwyer, Gerald P., Jr., and Hafer, R. W. *The Stock Market: Bubbles, Volatility, and Chaos*. Boston: Kluwer Academic Publishers, 1990.

Eichengreen, Barry. *Globalizing Capital*. Princeton: Princeton University Press, 1996.

Fagan, Brian. *The Long Summer*. New York: Basic Books, 2004.

Federal Reserve Bank of Kansas. *Financial Market Volatility and the Economy*. New York: Books for Business, 2001.

Fields, Gary. *Territories of Profit*. Stanford: Stanford Business Books, 2004.

Fischer, David Hackett. *The Great Wave*. New York: Oxford University Press, 1996.

Frank, Robert H., and Cook, Philip J. *The Winner-Take-All Society*. New York: The Free Press, 1995.

Friedman, Milton. *Money Mischief*. New York: Harcourt Brace & Company, 1994.

Friedman, Milton, and Schwartz, Anna Jacobson. *A Monetary History of the United States, 1867–1960*. Princeton: Princeton University Press, 1963.

Friedman, Thomas L. *Hot, Flat, and Crowded*. New York: Farrar, Straus and Giroux 2008.

——. *The World Is Flat*. New York: Farrar, Straus and Giroux, 2005.

Fukuyama, Francis. *The End of History and the Last Man*. New York: The Free Press, 1992.

——. *Trust*. New York: The Free Press, 1995.

Galbraith, John Kenneth. *Money*. New York: Houghton Mifflin Company, 1995.

——. *The Great Crash—1929*. New York: Houghton Mifflin Company, 1997.

Gardner, Mark R., and Ashby, W. Ross. "Connectance of Large Dynamic (Cybernetic) Systems: Critical Values for Stability." *Nature* 228 (21 November 1970).

Garrett, Laurie. *The Coming Plague*. London: Penguin Books, 1994.

Gimpel, Jean. *The Medieval Machine*. New York: Penguin Books, 1976.

Gladwell, Malcolm. *The Tipping Point*. New York: Little Brown and Company, 2000.

Gleick, James. *Chaos*. London: Penguin Books, 1987.

Godwin, Mike. *Cyber Rights*. New York: Times Books, 1998.

Gordon, Deborah. *Ants at Work*. New York: The Free Press, 1999.

Gray, John. *False Dawn*. New York: The New Press, 1998.

Green, Joshua. "The Amazing Money Machine." *The Atlantic*, June 2008, p. 62.

Grossman, Lawrence K. *The Electronic Republic*. New York: Viking, 1995.

Guehenno, Jean-Marie. *The End of the Nation-State*. Minneapolis: University of Minnesota Press, 1995.

Hafner, Katie, and Lyon, Matthew. *Where Wizards Stay Up Late*. New York: Simon and Schuster, 1996.

Hafner, Katie. *The Well*. New York: Carroll and Graf Publishers, 2001.

——, "The Internet's Invisible Hand; At a Public Utility Serving the World, No One's Really in Charge. Does It Matter?" *The New York Times*, January 10, 2002.

——, "Laurels For Giving the Internet Its Language." *The New York Times*, February 16, 2005.

Hardin, Garrett. *Living Within Limits*. Oxford: Oxford University Press, 1993.

Harper, Christopher. *And That's the Way It Will Be*. New York: New York University Press, 1998.

Harris, J. R. *Industrial Espionage and Technology Transfer*. Aldershot, U.K.: Ashgate, 1998.

Harvey, David. *The Condition of Postmodernity*. Cambridge, MA: Blackwell, 1990.

Hatfield, Elaine; Cacioppo, John T.; and Rapson, Richard L. *Emotional Contagion*. Cambridge: Cambridge University Press, 1994.

Hayek, F. A. *Denationalisation of Money*. London: The Institute of Economic Affairs, 1990.

Headrick, Daniel R. *When Information Came of Age*. Oxford: Oxford University Press, 2000.

Heilbroner, Robert L. *The Worldly Philosophers*. New York: Simon and Schuster, 1986.

Hempel, Sandra. *The Strange Case of the Broad Street Pump*. Berkeley: The University of California Press, 2007.

Hobsbawm, Eric. *The Age of Extremes*. New York: Vintage Books, 1994.

Hodgson, Geoffrey M. *Economics and Evolution*. Ann Arbor: University of Michigan Press, 1993.

Hogg, T.; Huberman, B. A.; and McGlade, Jacqueline M. *The Stability of Ecosystems*. Proceedings of the Royal Society of London, B 237,1989.

Hogg, Tad, and Huberman, Bernardo A. *Communities of Practice: Performance and Evolution, Computational and Mathematical Organizational Theory 1:1*. Hingham, MA: Kluwer Academic Publishers, 1995.

Holzmann, Gerald J., and Pehrson, Bjorn. *The Early History of Data Networks*. Hoboken, NJ: Wiley InterScience, 2003.

Horan, Thomas A. *Digital Places*. Washington, D.C.: Urban Land Institute, 2000.

Hull, John C. *Options, Futures, and Other Derivatives*. Upper Saddle River, NJ: Prentice Hall, 2000.

Jackson, Kenneth T. *Crabgrass Frontier*. New York: Oxford University Press, 1985.

Jacobs, Jane. *The Life and Death of Great American Cities*. New York: Vintage Books, 1992.

——. *The Nature of Economies*. New York: Vintage Books, 2000.

Johnson, Steven. *Emergence*. New York: Scribner, 2001.

Jonsson, Asgeir. *Why Iceland?* New York: McGraw Hill, 2009.

Kaplan, Robert D. *An Empire Wilderness*. New York: Random House, 1998.

——. *The Coming Anarchy*. New York: Random House, 2000.

Kelly, Kevin. *New Rules for the New Economy*. New York: Penguin Putnam Inc., 1998.

Keynes, John Maynard. *The General Theory of Employment, Interest, and Money*. New York: Harcourt, Brace, Jovanovich, 1953.

Kindleberger, Charles P., and Aliber, Robert. *Manias, Panics, and Crashes*. Hoboken, NJ: John Wiley and Sons, 2005.

Kohn, L. T.; Corrigan, J. M.; and Donaldson, M. S., eds. *To Err Is Human: Building a Safer Health System*. Washington, D.C.: National Academy Press, 1999.

Korten, David C. *When Corporations Rule the World*. San Francisco: Berrett-Koehler Publishers, 1995.

Krugman, Paul R. *Currencies and Crises* Cambridge, MA: MIT Press, 1999.

Kuhn, Thomas S. *The Structure of Scientific Revolutions*. Chicago: University of Chicago Press, 1970.

Kurtzman, Joe. *The Death of Money*. New York: Simon and Schuster, 1993.

Langewiesche, William. "The Lessons of ValuJet 592." *Atlantic Monthly*, March 1998.

Lansing, J. Stephen, and Miller, John H. "Cooperation in Balinese Rice Farming." Santa Fe Institute, May 30, 2003.

Lansing, J. Stephen. *Priests and Programmers: Technologies of Power in the Engineered Landscape of Bali*. Princeton: Princeton University Press, 1991.

Laszlo, Veres, and Woodman, Richard. *The Story of Sail*. Annapolis: Naval Institute Press, 1999.

Lewis, Michael. "Wall Street on the Tundra." *Vanity Fair*, April 2009.

Levitt, Steven D., and Dubner, Stephen J. *Freakonomics*. New York: William Morrow, 2005.

Lindblom, Charles E. "The Science of Muddling Through." *Public Administration Review,* vol. 19, pp. 79–88, 1959.

Lindblom, Charles E., *The Market System*. New Haven: Yale University Press, 2001.

Linden, Eugene. *The Future in Plain Sight*. New York: Simon and Schuster, 1998.

Lynch, Aaron. *Thought Contagion*. New York: Basic Books, 1996.

Mackay, Charles. *Extraordinary Popular Delusions and the Madness of Crowds*. New York: Metrobooks, 2002.

Mander, Jerry, and Goldsmith, Edward. *The Case Against the Global Economy*. San Francisco: Sierra Club Books, 1996.

Mankiw, N. Gregory. *Macroeconomics,* 3rd ed. New York: Worth Publishers, 1997.

Marglin, Stephen A. *The Dismal Science*. Cambridge, MA: Harvard University Press, 2008.

McMillan, John. *Reinventing the Bazaar*. New York: W.W. Norton and Company, 2002.

Merton, Robert K. *Social Theory and Structure*. New York: The Free Press, 1968.

Microbial Threats to Health. eds. Mark S. Smolinski, Margaret Hamburg, Joshua Lederberg. Washington, D.C.: National Academies Press, 2003.

Mitchell, William J. *e-topia*. Cambridge, MA: MIT Press, 1999.

——. *Me++ The Cyborg Self and the Networked City*. Cambridge, MA: MIT Press, 2003.

——. *City of Bits*. Cambridge, MA: MIT Press, 1996.

Mokyr, Joel. *The British Industrial Revolution*. Boulder: Westview Press, 1993.

——. *The Gifts of Athena: Historical Origins of the Knowledge Economy*. Princeton: Princeton University Press, 2002.

——. *The Lever of Riches*. Oxford: Oxford University Press, 1990.

Morowitz, Harold J. *The Emergence of Everything*. Oxford: Oxford University Press, 2002.

Mumford, Lewis. *Technics and Civilization*. New York: Harcourt Brace and Company, 1934.

——. *The City in History*. New York: Harcourt Brace and Company, 1961.

North, Douglass C. *Structure and Change in Economic History*. New York: W.W. Norton, 1981.

O'Harrow, Robert, Jr. *No Place To Hide*. New York: The Free Press, 2005.

Ogburn, William F. *On Culture and Social Change*. Chicago: University of Chicago Press, 1964.

Ohmae, Kenichi. *The End of the Nation State*. New York: The Free Press, 1995.

Orbe, Mark P., and Harris, Tina M. *Interracial Communication: Theory Into Practice*, 2nd ed. Thousand Oaks, CA: Sage Publications, 2007.

Palumbi, Stephen R. *The Evolution Explosion*. New York: W.W. Norton, 2001.

Parker, Ian. "Letter from Reykjavik," *The New Yorker*, March 9, 2009.

Perrow, Charles. *Normal Accidents*. Princeton: Princeton University Press, 1999.

Pettifor, Ann. *The Coming First World Debt Crisis*. New York: Palgrave Macmillan, 2006.

Piel, Gerard. *The Acceleration of History*. New York: Alfred A. Knopf 1972.

Pinker, Steven. *The Blank Slate: The Modern Denial of Human Nature*. New York: Viking, 2002.

Pinkerton, James P. *What Comes Next*. New York: Hyperion, 1995.

Popper, Karl. *The Poverty of Historicism*. London: Routledge Classics, 2002.

Putnam, Robert D. *Bowling Alone*. New York: Simon and Schuster, 2002.

——. *Making Democracy Work*. Princeton: Princeton University Press, 1993.

Reed, Robert C. *Train Wrecks*. Atglen, PA: Schiffer Publishing, Ltd., 1968.

Reeves, Byron, and Nass, Clifford. *The Media Equation*. Cambridge: Cambridge University Press, 1996.

Rheingold, Howard. *Smart Mobs*. New York: Basic Books, 2002.

Ricardo, David. *On the Principles of Political Economy and Taxation*. Kitchener, Ontario: Batoche Books, 2001. socserv2.socsci.mcmaster.ca/~econ/ugcm/3ll3/ricardo/Principles.pdf

Rochlin, Gene I. *Trapped in the Net*. Princeton: Princeton University Press, 1997.

Rohlfs, Jeffrey, H. *Bandwagon Effects*. Cambridge, MA: MIT Press, 2001.

Roll, Eric. *A History of Economic Thought*. London: Faber and Faber, 1938.

Romer, Paul M. "Economic Growth." *The Fortune Encyclopedia of Economics,* ed. David R. Henderson. New York: Warner Books, 1993.

Rosenberg, Nathan. *Exploring the Black Box*. Cambridge: Cambridge University Press, 1994.

——. *Inside the Black Box*. Cambridge: Cambridge University Press, 1982.

Rosenberg, Nathan, and Mowery, David C. *Paths of Innovation*. Cambridge: Cambridge University Press, 1998.

Rosenberg, Nathan. "Uncertainty and Technological Change." Prepared for the

Conference on Growth and Development: The Economics of the 21st Century, organized by the Center for Economic Policy Research of Stanford University, June 3–4, 1994.

Ruddiman, William F. *Plows, Plagues, and Petroleum*. Princeton: Princeton University Press, 2005.

Sagan, Scott D. *The Limits of Safety*. Princeton: Princeton University Press, 1993.

Saxenian, Annalee. *Regional Advantage*. Cambridge, MA: Harvard University Press, 1994.

Schivelbusch, Wolfgang. *The Railway Journey*. Berkeley: University of California Press, 1977.

Schott, Jeffrey J. *The WTO After Seattle*. Washington, D.C.: Institute for International Economics, 2000.

Scott, James C. *Seeing Like A State*. New Haven: Yale University Press, 1998.

Shelton, Judy. *Money Meltdown*. New York: The Free Press, 1994.

Slaughter, Anne-Marie. *A New World Order*. Princeton: Princeton University Press, 2004.

Slouka, Mark. *War of the Worlds*. New York: Basic Books, 1995.

Smith, Adam. *The Wealth of Nations*. London: Penguin Classics,1986.

Solomon, Elinor Harris. *Virtual Money*. Oxford: Oxford University Press, 1997.

Sornette, Didier. *Why Stock Markets Crash*. Princeton: Princeton University Press, 2003.

Spufford, Peter. *Power and Profit: The Merchant in Medieval Europe*. New York: Thames & Hudson, 2002.

Standage, Tom. *The Victorian Internet*. New York: Berkley Publishing Co., 1998.

Stiglitz, Joseph E. *Globalization and Its Discontents*. New York: W.W. Norton, 2002.

Stokes, Gale. *The Walls Came Tumbling Down*. Oxford: Oxford University Press, 1993.

Stuart, Guy. *Discriminating Risk: The U.S. Mortgage Lending Industry in the Twentieth Century*. Ithaca, New York: Cornell University Press, 2003.

Sykes, Charles J. *The End of Privacy*. New York: St. Martin's Griffin, 1999.

Tapscott, Don. *Growing Up Digital*. New York: McGraw Hill, 1998.

Taylor, John B. *Getting Off Track*. Stanford: Hoover Institution Press, 2009.

Tenner, Edward. *Why Things Bite Back*. New York: Vintage Books, 1997.

The Boston Consulting Group. *Perspectives on Experience*, 1968.

Thubron, Colin. *The Ancient Mariners*. Alexandria, VA: Time-Life Books, 1981.

Turkle, Sherry. *Life on the Screen*. New York: Simon and Schuster, 1995.

Vaughan, Diane. *The Challenger Launch Decision*. Chicago: University of Chicago Press, 1997.

Wachter, Robert M., and Shojania, Kaveh G. *Internal Bleeding*. New York: Rugged Land, 2004.

Waldrop, M. Mitchell. *Complexity*. New York: Touchstone, 1993.

Wallace, Jonathan, and Mangan, Mark. *Sex, Laws, and Cyberspace*. Henry Holt & Co., 1996.

Wallace, Patricia. *The Psychology of the Internet*. Cambridge: Cambridge University Press, 1999.

Ward, Diane Raines. *Water Wars*. New York: Penguin Putnam, 2002.

Warner, Sam Bass, Jr. *Streetcar Suburbs*. Cambridge, MA: Harvard University Press,

1978.

Warsh, David. *Knowledge and the Wealth of Nations*. New York: W.W. Norton, 2006.

Watts, Duncan J. *Six Degrees*. New York: W.W. Norton, 2003.

——. *Small Worlds*. Princeton: Princeton University Press, 2004.

White, Lynn, Jr. *Medieval Technology and Social Change*. Oxford: Oxford University Press, 1964.

Wigner, E. P. "On the Distribution of the Roots of Certain Symmetric Matrices." *Annals Math* 67 (1958): 325–327.

Wilson, James Q., and Keeling, George L. "Broken Windows." *Atlantic Monthly*, March 1982, pp. 29–38.

Wolfe, Tom. "The Tinkerings of Robert Noyce: How the Sun Rose on Silicon Valley." *Esquire Magazine*, December 1983.

Womack, James P.; Jones, Daniel T.; and Roos, Daniel. *The Machine That Changed The World*. New York: Rawson Associates, 1990.

Wright, Robert, *Non Zero,* New York: Pantheon Books, 2002.

Wriston, Walter B. *The Twilight of Sovereignty*. New York: Charles Scribner's Sons, 1992.

Yergin, Daniel, and Stanislaw, Joseph. *The Commanding Heights*. New York: Simon and Schuster, 1998.

Index

About the Author

William H. Davidow is a successful Silicon Valley venture capitalist, philanthropist, and author. As a senior vice president of Intel Corporation, he was responsible for the design of the Intel microprocessor chip. He has written three previous books—*Marketing High Technology* (The Free Press, 1986), *Total Customer Service* (HarperCollins, 1989), with Bro Uttal, and *The Virtual Corporation* (HarperCollins, 1992), with Michael Malone—as well as columns for *Forbes* and numerous op-ed pieces. He graduated from Dartmouth College and has a master's degree from the California Institute of Technology and a Ph.D. from Stanford University. He serves on the boards of CalTech, the California Nature Conservancy, and the Stanford Institute for Economic Policy Research.